180 Prayers

COURAGEOUS GIRL

180 Prayers

COURAGEOUS GIRL

Quiet-Time Inspiration
& Encouragement

Janice
Thompson

BARBOUR kidz

Print ISBN 978-1-63609-191-4

Published by Barbour Publishing, Inc., 1810 Barbour Drive, Uhrichsville, Ohio 44683, www.barbourbooks.com

Our mission is to inspire the world with the life-changing message of the Bible.

Printed in the United States of America.

001109 0322 SP

Introduction

God is interested in every single thing you have to say, courageous girl!

In fact, He loves when His daughters take the time to talk to Him. You've got a lot on your mind, and His ears are wide open. This devotional prayer book is a great reminder to chat with your heavenly Father about anything and everything on your mind.

Maybe you can't stop thinking about that girl in your language arts class, the one who looks so sad. Maybe you're having trouble forgiving that boy on the playground who hurt your feelings. Maybe you're worried about a grandmother who's sick or a friend who doesn't know Jesus. Whether you're happy or sad, excited or down in the dumps, you'll find prayers in this book that will hit the spot. Each prayer is perfectly paired with a great verse from the Bible—a totally fabulous way for you to begin or end your day.

Quiet time with your heavenly Father is the best! He can't wait to hang out with you. So what's keeping you? Dive on in! Let's start praying.

You've seen it all, haven't you? The awesome, the not so great, and the icky! Some friendships are harder than others. But nothing is impossible with God. So talk to Him about all of your friendships, and then watch Him turn even the icky ones around!

My Friends

Jesus, thank You for my friends! The tall ones, short ones, chatty ones, shy ones, goofy ones, quiet ones. . . I love them all, and I'm happy they're in my life. Even on the bad days, my friends know how to make me laugh. When I'm feeling down, they make me forget about my troubles. They tell me jokes, and I get the giggles. They blow bubbles with their gum. They act goofy so I won't be upset anymore. Sometimes they just sit and listen when I tell them what I'm going through. I like that best of all. I don't know where I'd be without my friends, Lord. Show me how to be the kind of friend others have been to me so that I can be a shining reflection of You in this world. I want to be the best friend I can be. Amen.

A man of many companions may come to ruin, but there is a friend who sticks closer than a brother.

PROVERBS 18:24 ESV

Dare to Be Different

I don't know why I work so hard to be like my friends, Lord. You didn't create us to be cookie-cutter creations, after all! What does it really matter if I dress differently or wear my hair in my own style? Sometimes it's cooler to stand out in the crowd, to be unique. Give me the courage to be myself. I don't want to be a follower. I want to be a leader, one who dares to be exactly who she's supposed to be. When others are saying mean or hurtful things to kids around them, help me behave differently. I don't just want to *look* different; I want to *be* different. Help me, I pray. Amen.

Finally, dear brothers and sisters, we urge you in the name of the Lord Jesus to live in a way that pleases God, as we have taught you. You live this way already, and we encourage you to do so even more.

1 THESSALONIANS 4:1 NLT

Accountability

Sometimes, Lord, I need an accountability partner—someone who holds me responsible, someone who says, "Hey, did you do that thing you said you were gonna do?" I don't always follow through on my own, but with the help of a friend, maybe I'd do a better job. Can You show me which friend would make a good partner? And while we're at it, could You help me be that kind of friend to others? I want to be the sort of person others can turn to when they need a reminder. Most of all, I'm thankful that You hold me accountable, Lord. You're always whispering in my ear, "Hey, remember to clean your room!" or "Don't forget to do your homework." Best accountability partner ever! Amen.

Brothers, if anyone is caught in any transgression, you who are spiritual should restore him in a spirit of gentleness. Keep watch on yourself, lest you too be tempted. Bear one another's burdens, and so fulfill the law of Christ.

GALATIANS 6:1–2 ESV

Popularity

I wish there was no such word as *popular*, Lord. It's a bad word to me, because it makes some people feel like they're better than others, just because of the way they look or the clothes they wear or the friends they have. It pushes other people away and causes some girls to think they are more important. In Your eyes, we're all the same! You created us equal, so no one is popular or unpopular according to You. You see us all the same—no matter what we look like or who we hang out with. Help me to treat everyone the same, just like You do, Lord. And when the "popular" girls are up to their tricks, remind me that the only opinion that matters is Yours. Amen.

You are judging by appearances. If anyone is confident that they belong to Christ, they should consider again that we belong to Christ just as much as they do.

2 CORINTHIANS 10:7 NIV

A Friend to the Friendless

I don't always feel like I have a lot of friends, Lord. And sometimes I wonder if the girls who pretend to be my friends really are. (Sometimes their actions don't line up with their words!) I know what it's like to feel left out, which is why my heart really hurts when I see girls who are excluded on purpose. They don't get picked to be in the group because they're different. It's not right, Lord. No one should be left out. . .for any reason. Today, give me the courage to be the sort of girl who goes out of her way to include everyone. I can do it with Your help, Lord. I know You love everyone just the same—and I do too. Amen.

So let's stop condemning each other. Decide instead to live in such a way that you will not cause another believer to stumble and fall.

ROMANS 14:13 NLT

Healthy Relationships

Lord, You know I've had a few rocky friendships. There are some girls out there who make things difficult. They aren't always honest, and sometimes they do things to hurt me. But I'm learning to make good choices, Father! I want to have friends who treat others kindly and who help me grow in my faith. Would You bring new friends like this into my life, Lord? I really need them. Please send me strong, sweet friends who will bring out the best in me. I want my relationships to be healthy, Lord, and I want to be the very best friend I can possibly be to others. Amen.

Let your conversation be gracious and attractive so that you will have the right response for everyone.

COLOSSIANS 4:6 NLT

Friend Drama

I'm not a fan of drama, Lord, especially when it involves my friends. This one can't stand that one. This one's mad at that one. This one's gossiping about that one behind her back. That one says she'll never hang out with the group again if we don't get rid of the girl she can't stand. *Ugh!* It's so hard not to get caught up in all the chaos! That's why I need Your help. When my friends are creating drama, show me how to be a peacemaker. Teach me how to stay out of it so that things don't get worse. I want to be a good friend to everyone in my group, so show me how to rise above the drama, I pray. Amen.

Above all, clothe yourselves with love, which binds us all together in perfect harmony. And let the peace that comes from Christ rule in your hearts. For as members of one body you are called to live in peace. And always be thankful.

COLOSSIANS 3:14–15 NLT

Friend Envy

I'll admit it, Lord—sometimes I get jealous. In fact, I get so green with envy that I end up angry. Sometimes I'm jealous of the way other girls look or the pretty clothes they wear. Other times I'm jealous because my friend is super-talented, and I don't feel talented at all. Sometimes I wish I had the kind of life that others have. I envy their homes, cars, or vacations. I even get envious when my friends spend time together but don't ask me to join them. But then You remind me that I'm already blessed. I have all I need and more. There's no point in being jealous of others. I'm so glad for that reminder, Lord, because I don't want to be envious. Help me, please. Amen.

Anger is cruel and fury overwhelming,
but who can stand before jealousy?

PROVERBS 27:4 NIV

Kindness

I love when people are kind to me, Lord! It makes my heart smile when they go out of their way to treat me well. Sometimes all it takes is a smile or a nod and my day is made! Funny how a bad mood can change in a hurry when someone smiles at you! I want to be that sort of friend to others. May I be known for my kindness. When others look at me, I want them to say, "Oh, I know her! She's the one with the sweet attitude who always treats everyone so well." Today, show me how I can bless someone else with a kind deed. Make it creative, Lord! I want to bring a smile to a friend or loved one's face. Can You help me come up with a really fun idea, Lord? It's going to be great. I just know it! Amen.

Love never hurts a neighbor,
so loving is obeying all the law.

ROMANS 13:10 NCV

Others-Focused

I don't mean to think I'm better than other people, Lord. I don't do it on purpose. But many times, I put my wishes and desires above theirs. I care more about what I want than what they need. I like to get my own way. Let's face it: sometimes I'm a little selfish. Today, please show me how to think more highly of my friends and loved ones and to lay down my self-centered desires. I want to be others-focused, not self-focused. Would You help me with this, please? I sure can't do it on my own, Lord. Amen.

Do nothing from selfish ambition or conceit, but in humility count others more significant than yourselves.

PHILIPPIANS 2:3 ESV

FAMILY

Parents, siblings, grandparents, aunts, uncles, cousins. . . you're part of a great big family. God didn't place you where you are by accident. Nope! He knew exactly what He was doing! Whether they're goofy, cranky, or wacky, your family members are your people, and they adore you.

The Family You're In

You created families, Lord! What a cool idea! You decided there should be moms, dads, brothers, sisters, cousins, aunts, and uncles. You were especially creative when You thought up grandparents! Sometimes I wonder how I ended up in the family I'm in. I feel different from the others. But You put me here on purpose. I'm surrounded by exactly the right people, even when it doesn't feel like it. Today, please be with people who don't have families—elderly people, orphans, and widows. Show us who we can "adopt" into our family today. Amen.

For if someone does not know how to manage his own household, how will he care for God's church?

1 TIMOTHY 3:5 ESV

Parents

Lord, I think it's so cool that You decided to place kids in families. If I didn't have a mom or dad, who would have changed my diaper when I was little? Who would have fed me? You gave those jobs to people who love me and want to see me grow up healthy and strong. Have I thanked You lately for my parents? I don't always act like I'm grateful for them, but I am! They do so much for me—they make sure I have a safe place to live, a bed, good food, and clothes to wear. They work hard so that I can have a good life. I'm learning as I watch them. One day I want to be a great parent too. And by the way, thanks for being the very best Daddy ever, Lord. Amen!

Children, you belong to the Lord, and you do the right thing when you obey your parents. The first commandment with a promise says, "Obey your father and your mother, and you will have a long and happy life."

EPHESIANS 6:1–3 CEV

Grandparents

I love my grandparents, Lord! It's not just because they sometimes let me get away with things my parents don't. Okay, in all honesty, they do go easier on me! It's mostly because they love hanging out with me. We do such fun things together—play games, go to the park, go out to eat—lots of stuff that makes my heart happy. Mostly, I love talking to them. Their stories are the best! When they start talking about the things they did when they were kids, I feel like I'm watching a movie. Maybe one day I'll be a grandparent and I'll have cool stories to tell. How awesome would that be? If that happens, I hope I'm as much fun as my grandparents are right now. Thanks for giving them to me, Lord. Amen.

Grandchildren are the crown of the aged,
and the glory of children is their fathers.

PROVERBS 17:6 ESV

Siblings

Sometimes they sure get on my nerves, Lord. Brothers and sisters can be a real pain. Other times they're my BFFs. I love them so much. We play together and get into mischief together, and we're growing up together. I don't know why You chose to place me in the family You did, but it's been super-exciting. Help me to be the best sister I can be—to my real brothers and sisters and to those who are so close they're almost like family. I want to love others the way You do, Lord. I want to put their needs before my own. This is hard, but I want to give it my best shot. I'll need Your help if I'm going to succeed. May I win the Sister of the Year award! Amen.

Love each other like brothers and sisters. Give each other more honor than you want for yourselves.

ROMANS 12:10 NCV

Blended Families

You sure know how to bring people together, Lord! You can take broken families and mend them. You can bring in new brothers and sisters—halves and steps—and make them all whole. You love when we all live together in peace and harmony. Today I pray for everyone I know in a blended family, with new sisters, brothers, mothers, or fathers. May they all feel a sense of love and belonging. And thank You, Lord, for making us all part of Your family—no matter who we are, where we come from, or what we look like. We're all precious in Your sight, and that makes my heart happy! Thank You. Amen.

We ought always to give thanks to God for you, brothers, as is right, because your faith is growing abundantly, and the love of every one of you for one another is increasing.

2 THESSALONIANS 1:3 ESV

Church

A good church is like a family, isn't it, Lord? I have brothers and sisters (and tons of parents!) at my church. I'm surrounded on every side. There are people who love me like one of their own, and that feels so good. I love hanging out with the people at church because we can all worship You as one big happy family. And my church is a great community. I feel safe when I'm spending time with people there. Thanks for adding to the family, Lord. Amen.

And let us consider how to stir up one another to love and good works, not neglecting to meet together, as is the habit of some, but encouraging one another, and all the more as you see the Day drawing near.

HEBREWS 10:24–25 ESV

Divorce

Father, I've seen it so many times: parents splitting up. Kids getting hurt. Being caught in the middle. It's a terrible thing to have to divide your heart. Today I pray for every friend or loved one who's been through a divorce. For every child who's feeling guilty, who thinks it might be their fault, show them it's not. Heal every broken heart. Mend the hurt places. Give peace. Let them know that this isn't the end of a relationship with Mom or Dad, just the beginning of a new and different one. You can mend anything, Lord, even a heart shattered by divorce. Thank You for caring about parents and kids dealing with divorce. Amen.

Two are better than one, because they have a good reward for their toil. For if they fall, one will lift up his fellow. But woe to him who is alone when he falls and has not another to lift him up! Again, if two lie together, they keep warm, but how can one keep warm alone? And though a man might prevail against one who is alone, two will withstand him—a threefold cord is not quickly broken.

ECCLESIASTES 4:9–12 ESV

One Big Happy Family

I hear that expression a lot, Lord—"one big happy family." Only, we're not always happy. It seems like someone's always upset or mad. One kid is jealous of the other. Mom's frustrated. Dad's tired from working all day. We have days that totally stink! Then on other days, everything goes right. My brothers and sisters are in a good mood, Mom has a smile on her face, and Dad is happy to have a day off from work. In good times and bad, I know You're there for us, Lord. And in spite of any rough days, we really are one big happy family. . .because we have one another. Thanks for sticking with us, Lord. Amen.

"Your offspring shall be like the dust of the earth, and you shall spread abroad to the west and to the east and to the north and to the south, and in you and your offspring shall all the families of the earth be blessed."

GENESIS 28:14 ESV

Don't Mess with My Family!

Lord, I don't like people messing with my family. When bullies start picking on my brother or sister, I get mad. And when my mom is crying because someone hurt her feelings, it breaks my heart. I just want to protect those I love. I know You understand how I feel. You're the best protector of all! You don't like people messing with Your kids. You love and defend us whenever we're in trouble. Help me not to lose my temper or do the wrong thing when I'm upset. I want to show love, even to those who pick on us, so that they can see Your light shining through my life. Help me, I pray. Amen.

Say to your brothers, "You are my people," and to your sisters, "You have received mercy."

HOSEA 2:1 ESV

Part of a Bigger Family

Sometimes I like to think about my family—not just the people in my house, but my aunts, uncles, cousins, grandparents, and so on. I even like to imagine what my great-grandparents and their relatives must have been like. Do I look or act like any of them, Lord? I'm just curious. The truth is, I come from a super-huge family, one that goes back generations. Before I was even born, people in my family were praying for me. I can just imagine my great-grandmother praying for all of the children to come. Wow! I want to be like that, Lord. Even now, while I'm young, I lift up my future children, grandchildren, and great-grandchildren to You! I love being part of such a big, amazing family. May we all live to serve and love You. Amen.

And he took them the same hour of the night and washed their wounds; and he was baptized at once, he and all his family.

ACTS 16:33 ESV

RELATIONSHIP WITH GOD

It's the most important relationship you'll ever have—your one-on-one relationship with your heavenly Father! You can't borrow this relationship from your mom or dad. You have to experience it on your own. And it starts with spending time with Him. Why wait? He has His hand out right now, inviting you to sit awhile and visit.

God, My Father

You're my Father! I love it! You're the Father of all of us, so we're one big happy family. You love us in the way that a daddy would—with tender compassion and joy. You love to see Your kids laugh, smile, and get along. That's what all dads want. Most of all, You love spending time with me. You love when I take the time to read my Bible and pray. That's our special one-on-one time, just You and me. Thanks for looking out for me, for protecting me and caring so much about what happens in my life. You're a great heavenly Father, and I'm so happy to be Your daughter. Amen.

Yet for us there is one God, the Father, from whom are all things and for whom we exist, and one Lord, Jesus Christ, through whom are all things and through whom we exist.

1 CORINTHIANS 8:6 ESV

God's Ways Are Higher

I always think I know the best way to do things, Lord. I can be a real know-it-all sometimes. But I'm figuring out that You know best. When I don't get my way and I feel like stamping my foot or complaining, You whisper, *"I've got something better!"* in my ear. Today I choose to trust You even when things don't seem to be working out. Even when my friend won't speak to me. Even when my prayers aren't answered the way I think they should be. I'll trust in You because I know You have bigger, better things coming. I can't wait to see what You have in store for me, Lord. Amen.

Now to him who is able to do immeasurably more than all we ask or imagine, according to his power that is at work within us, to him be glory in the church and in Christ Jesus throughout all generations, for ever and ever! Amen.

EPHESIANS 3:20–21 NIV

A Girl after God's Own Heart

I chase after so many things, Lord—friends, sports, cool clothes, even good grades. But the truth is, I only need to chase after You and You'll take care of all those things. If I want a better life, I need to start with a stronger relationship with You. So today I choose to draw close to You, to tell You that You mean everything to me—more than my friends, more than my cool stuff, even more than my hopes and wishes and dreams. You're my all in all, Jesus! I draw near to You, and I know You will take care of everything I need. I praise You for that. Amen.

The LORD appeared to us in the past, saying:
"I have loved you with an everlasting love;
I have drawn you with unfailing kindness."

JEREMIAH 31:3 NIV

Putting God First

Sometimes I forget that I should be putting You first, God. Your name should be the first name I speak when I wake up in the morning. Your thoughts and opinions should be the ones that matter most to me. I spend so much time worrying what other people think about me when I should be focused more on what You think. When I put You first in my life, everything else falls into place. Everything comes into order. Today I choose to make my relationship with You the most important thing. I can't wait to see how things come together. Amen.

"But seek first the kingdom of God and his righteousness, and all these things will be added to you."

MATTHEW 6:33 ESV

God's Word

I love my Bible, Lord! It's filled with so many cool stories from days gone by: Joseph and his amazing coat of many colors. Noah, a man of courage who followed Your orders, even though they didn't make sense at the time. Samson, a man of strength. David, a man who loved You with his whole heart. Mary, a young woman who became the mother of Jesus. The disciples, who chose to follow Jesus no matter what. I can learn so many lessons from these stories! They teach me how to be brave, how to stand up to my enemies, and how to love and serve You more. I'm so grateful for the Word of God! Thanks for sharing it with us, Lord. What a blessing! Amen.

For the word of God is alive and active. Sharper than any double-edged sword, it penetrates even to dividing soul and spirit, joints and marrow; it judges the thoughts and attitudes of the heart.

HEBREWS 4:12 NIV

Prayer Time

I love hanging out with You, Lord. I know I can tell You anything—the things I'm worried about, the things I love, even the things I'm hoping to do with my life. You're the best listener ever! Mostly, I love telling You how great You are. You're an awesome God! There's something so great about praising You. I could sing a song right now just to celebrate Your goodness! Thanks for always being there, Lord. Thanks for keeping Your door open and Your light on so that I can come any time of the day or night and tell You what I'm going through. I'm so grateful for the time we spend together. I love You, Lord! Amen.

Don't worry about anything; instead, pray about everything. Tell God what you need, and thank him for all he has done. Then you will experience God's peace, which exceeds anything we can understand. His peace will guard your hearts and minds as you live in Christ Jesus.

PHILIPPIANS 4:6–7 NLT

Worship

I haven't really understood this word *worship*, Lord. Sometimes I think it's part of our church service, when we sing songs. Other times I think it's when we pray or say words like, "I love You, Lord! I adore You!" Sometimes I think worship is how we live our lives as believers. So I read Your Word, and I see that it's all of the above! True worship is living a life that is totally devoted to You, Jesus. When I put You first, the songs I sing, the prayers I pray, the words of devotion I speak, the way I talk to others, the way I dress, the people I hang out with. . .all of those things become an act of worship. Today I choose to be completely devoted! May my whole life be an act of worship, Lord. Amen.

Oh come, let us worship and bow down;
let us kneel before the LORD, our Maker!

PSALM 95:6 ESV

Hello, God. Are You There?

Okay, I have to admit something, Lord. Sometimes I wonder if You're really there. I pray to You, and I don't know if You hear me. I feel like my prayers are bouncing off the ceiling. Sometimes it even feels a little weird to pray to Someone I can't see with my own eyes. But that's when I need to trust. I need to believe, even when I can't see or feel Your presence. Your Word says You'll never leave me or forsake me. That means You're always with me even when it doesn't feel like it. Give me the faith and courage to believe even during those times, Lord. You're right there! Amen.

"Be strong and courageous. Do not fear or be in dread of them, for it is the LORD your God who goes with you. He will not leave you or forsake you."

DEUTERONOMY 31:6 ESV

Faith

I want to talk to You about this word *faith*, Lord. Mom says I need to have it, even when I can't see proof with my own eyes. Here's an example: When my grandma got sick and had to go in the hospital, it looked like she wouldn't make it. So I prayed. At first it didn't look like she was getting better. I really, truly started to believe in my heart that You could heal her if You wanted to. Grandma must've started believing it too, and she got well. You healed her. Show me how to believe, even when it feels impossible, Lord. I want to be a girl who has great faith in You. Amen.

Since we have been made right with God by our faith, we have peace with God. This happened through our Lord Jesus Christ, who through our faith has brought us into that blessing of God's grace that we now enjoy. And we are happy because of the hope we have of sharing God's glory.

ROMANS 5:1–2 NCV

The King's Daughter

I get it, Lord! I'm a daughter of the King! Because I'm Your daughter, I'm royalty. I can almost picture my beautiful tiara now! You chose me. You called me to live an amazing life as Your child. You've set me apart to do great things for You. May I live every day as a child You can be proud of, a princess with an excellent attitude. May I shine like a star for You, always doing or saying the things You would do or say. (That's what a true princess does, after all. She's a reflection of her father, the king.) Thanks for inviting me to be Your daughter, Lord. Amen.

But you are a chosen race, a royal priesthood, a holy nation, a people for his own possession, that you may proclaim the excellencies of him who called you out of darkness into his marvelous light.

1 PETER 2:9 ESV

ATTITUDE

Whether you're having a good day or bad, it's your attitude that counts! Maybe it's time to have a little chat with God about how you can have a better one.

A Good Attitude

I don't always have the best attitude, Lord. Some days I'm just in a bad mood. I don't really know why. Maybe because I'm tired or because of stuff going on at school. I'm sorry about my bad attitude. Help me to be a girl who's positive and upbeat. When others look at me, I don't want them to say, "Wow, her attitude really stinks!" Just the opposite! I want them to look at me and say, "I want to be like her. She always has a smile on her face." That can only happen if I stick close to You. You're the ultimate teacher when it comes to great attitudes. So today, I choose to be like You. Please help me, Lord. Amen.

Throw off your old sinful nature and your former way of life. . . . Instead, let the Spirit renew your thoughts and attitudes.

EPHESIANS 4:22–23 NLT

Is the Glass Half Full?

I love people who have a great attitude, Lord. They bring happiness to situations (even tough situations). They always see the glass as half full. I want to be a glass-half-full girl too, someone who sees the best and hopes for great things. I want to be positive and uplifting, someone who brings a smile to the faces of those around me. I know this kind of joy can only come from You, so today I ask You to give me a double dose. Amen.

Do everything without complaining and arguing, so that no one can criticize you. Live clean, innocent lives as children of God, shining like bright lights in a world full of crooked and perverse people. Hold firmly to the word of life; then, on the day of Christ's return, I will be proud that I did not run the race in vain and that my work was not useless.

PHILIPPIANS 2:14–16 NLT

Fabulous

A lot of girls think they're fabulous because they're pretty or have great hair. They think *fabulous* is a word to describe the clothes they wear or the girls they hang around with. A girl who's really fabulous is kindhearted and generous, one with a fabulous attitude no matter what she's facing. I want to be that kind of girl, Lord. My actions will reflect my heart if I'm fabulous all the way to the core. I know I can be, as long as I do my best to be like You. You're the most fabulous of all, Father, and I want to be like You. Today, will You help me with that? Amen.

"You are the light of the world. A town built on a hill cannot be hidden."

MATTHEW 5:14 NIV

Patience

I'm not very patient, Lord. When I want something, I want it now! Who wants to wait until Christmas to get the latest, greatest video game or bike? Talk about a bad attitude! Sometimes I forget that waiting can be a good thing. You are teaching me to be patient though, so I have to try. It wouldn't be good for me if I got everything I wanted right away anyway. I wouldn't appreciate things as much. I'd be spoiled. So I'll wait as patiently as I can for the things I hope to get one day. And while I'm waiting, I'll go ahead and thank You for all the things You've already blessed me with. What an amazing Father You are! Amen.

But if we hope for what we do not see, we wait for it with patience.

ROMANS 8:25 ESV

Humility

Lord, sometimes I forget to be humble. I get a little puffed up. My attitude kicks in. I brag about myself. I tell other people about all the cool stuff I've done—my good grades, my talents, my abilities. I show off. Oh, I'm not bragging on purpose. Sometimes I just forget that singing my own praises isn't the best way to get people to like me. Will You help me with this? Whenever I'm tempted to brag, remind me that all of my abilities come from You. They're not my own doing. If I'm going to brag on anyone, let me brag on You, Jesus! You're the best, after all. Amen.

Be completely humble and gentle; be patient, bearing with one another in love.

EPHESIANS 4:2 NIV

Temper, Temper!

I don't know where the anger comes from sometimes, Lord. I'm having a normal day, then—*bam!*—someone does something that sets me off like a rocket ship! Wow, do I know how to explode! I come out swinging and yelling, red in the face with anger. Oops. I don't mean to get angry. And I'm always embarrassed after it's over, especially when Mom or Dad or one of my teachers calls me out on it. Can You help me with my anger, Lord? I don't want to be known as the girl who blows up at people. I want to have a calm, loving spirit. . .a great attitude. Today I give You my anger and ask You to change my heart forever. Amen.

"In your anger do not sin": Do not let the sun go down while you are still angry, and do not give the devil a foothold.

EPHESIANS 4:26–27 NIV

Gentleness

I hear it all the time, Lord: "Be gentle!" It doesn't come easily for me, not just because I'm a kid, but because I have a ton of energy! Gentleness is something I have to work on. Show me how to be gentler—with my words, my actions, and my attitude. Sometimes my attitude gets a little out of hand! No matter how others are acting, I want to be a calm force. When they get crazy, I'll get calm. When Mom says, "Hey, cool it in there!" I actually will. I won't react with anger or frustration. With the help of Your Holy Spirit, I'll stay calm, cool, and collected. Thanks, Lord! Amen.

Always be humble, gentle, and patient,
accepting each other in love.

EPHESIANS 4:2 NCV

Respect

I'm learning what it means to treat others with respect. Sometimes it means that even if you disagree with them, you don't pitch a fit. I'm even learning what it means to respect the things I own. If I throw my dirty clothes on the floor, I'm not respecting them very much, am I? You want me to show respect all the time, not just when I'm in a good mood. That's a hard one, Lord, but I'm working on it! Help me, I pray. I want to be a girl who respects others and shows respect for her possessions too. Amen.

Love one another with brotherly affection.
Outdo one another in showing honor.

ROMANS 12:10 ESV

The Fruit of the Spirit

Dear Lord, to me, having the fruit of the Spirit is a sign of having a heart surrendered to You. I want to be known for my kindness, my gentleness, my self-control. I want others to see my love, my joy, my peace, my patience. I want my life to exhibit faithfulness and goodness. These are the fruits I want to share with the world. It isn't always easy, Lord. There are times when I choose anger, revenge, and bitterness. During those times, please remind me that a fruitful life is a stronger, healthier life. I want to be like You, Jesus! Help me to bear fruit. Amen.

But the fruit of the Spirit is love, joy, peace, patience, kindness, goodness, faithfulness, gentleness, self-control; against such things there is no law.

GALATIANS 5:22–23 ESV

Stuck Up

It's hard to be around people who are stuck up, Lord. You know the ones. . .with all the attitude. They really get on my nerves. They think they're better than everyone else. *Ugh.* I never know what to do when these people come along. Should I ignore them? Should I stop being friends with them? It's so hard to know sometimes. Show me how to love everyone, Father, even the ones who don't make it easy. When other girls ignore me or leave me out of their groups, help me not to be hurt or offended. Remind me that You always include me, and You want me to be the kind of girl who includes others. So that's what I'll do. No matter how others treat me, I'll be kind to all. Amen.

Talk no more so very proudly, let not arrogance come from your mouth; for the LORD is a God of knowledge, and by him actions are weighed.

1 SAMUEL 2:3 ESV

BEAUTIFUL IN HIM

You might not feel beautiful all the time, but to God, you're stunning! In fact, He thinks you're absolutely gorgeous, even on the bad hair days. Freckles? No problem. Chubby waistline? He doesn't care. He just wants you to know that you are loved by the King of kings.

Beauty

I don't always like what I see when I look in the mirror, Lord. I see freckles, messy hair, and mismatched clothes. My reflection isn't really who I am. I know that. Your Word says that I'm beautiful in Your sight, even on my messiest day. I want to be a girl who's lovely from the inside out. I want my words to be beautiful, my attitude to be sweet, and my heart to delight itself in You. In other words, I want to be more like You, Lord. I know You're better than any hairstylist or makeup artist. You really can make me beautiful deep down inside. You can take my bitterness, my pain, my anger, and replace them with love. Now that's a beautiful makeover! Amen.

You are altogether beautiful,
my love; there is no flaw in you.

SONG OF SOLOMON 4:7 ESV

Inner Beauty

Is it possible for someone to be really pretty on the inside but not so pretty on the outside? That's how I feel sometimes. I don't always like the reflection I see in the mirror, but I'm working extra-hard to make sure the inner girl is beautiful. I know so many girls who seem to have the reverse problem: they're pretty on the outside, but they don't treat others nicely. It's weird to see how their beauty seems to fade as ugly words come out. I might never be a beauty queen on the outside, Lord, but feel free to turn me into one on the inside. I want Your love, joy, and peace to shine through, no matter where I am or what I'm doing. Amen.

Do not let your adorning be external—the braiding of hair and the putting on of gold jewelry, or the clothing you wear—but let your adorning be the hidden person of the heart with the imperishable beauty of a gentle and quiet spirit, which in God's sight is very precious.

1 PETER 3:3–4 ESV

In Style

Some girls care way too much about style, Lord. They spend too much time looking in the mirror—focusing on their hair, their clothes, their skin, or their figure. Me? I think it's cool to be stylish, but that's not the most important thing. The best sort of style is a great attitude. What good would it do to wear cool clothes if you have a bad attitude after all? So I'll work on my inner style, while others are focused on their outer style. Before long, with Your help, I'll be able to do an inside-out style show! Amen.

Therefore, as God's chosen people, holy and dearly loved, clothe yourselves with compassion, kindness, humility, gentleness and patience.

COLOSSIANS 3:12 NIV

Comparison

It's so hard not to compare myself to others, Lord. I see a girl with beautiful, perfect hair, and I'm disappointed in how my hair looks. I notice a friend has a new outfit, and I wish I could have one. If only I looked as cute as she does. If only my life were as easy as hers. Truth is, I know that no one really has a perfect life. It might look like it from the outside, but everyone has struggles. Today I choose to be happy with who I am. I won't compare myself with others. I'll be content, no matter what. Amen.

We do not dare to compare ourselves with those who think they are very important. They use themselves to measure themselves, and they judge themselves by what they themselves are. This shows that they know nothing.

2 CORINTHIANS 10:12 NCV

Identity in Christ

Sometimes I look in the mirror and wonder who I am. Do I matter? Do I have value? Or am I just another kid, one who won't make a difference in this world? Then I'm reminded of what the Bible says—I'm Your child! I'm called by Your name. I'm a brand-new person when I ask Jesus to come into my heart. You're my Daddy, and I'm Your daughter—a princess in Your eyes. So when I look in the mirror today, don't let me get distracted by how I look or by the clothes I wear. Remind me that I'm Yours, Lord. My identity is in You! Amen.

Therefore, if anyone is in Christ, he is a new creation. The old has passed away; behold, the new has come.

2 CORINTHIANS 5:17 ESV

Body Image

Why do I always feel like I have to be perfect, Lord? I feel like I won't fit in unless I have the perfect hair or skin color. I wonder if people will like me because my nose is shaped funny or I have a mole on my arm. I think my hips are too big or my thighs are too chubby. In other words, I overthink things based on how I look. I have a messed-up body image. Can You change my thinking? Can You remind me every day that I'm exactly the girl You created me to be? Whether I'm thin or chubby, short or tall, dark-skinned or light. . .I'm exactly who You created me to be, and You don't make mistakes. I can rest in the truth: You adore me just as I am! Amen.

For you created my inmost being; you knit me together in my mother's womb. I praise you because I am fearfully and wonderfully made; your works are wonderful, I know that full well.

PSALM 139:13–14 NIV

Glamour

My friends are so into the glamour scene, Lord. They look on Instagram to check out makeup, hairstyles, cool clothes, and even dieting tips. But I don't care a lot about all that. I mean, I know someday it'll probably be more important to me, but right now I want to stay focused on what it means to live a glamorous life for You. I want my life, my actions, my attitude, to be beautiful in Your sight. Even if I'm a mess on the outside (and some days I am), I want my heart to reflect godly glamour, to be lovely and attractive, not just to You, but to everyone I meet. I want people to say, "Wow, she's a glamorous girl who really loves Jesus!" Help me with that, I pray. Amen.

Charm is deceitful, and beauty is vain, but a woman who fears the LORD is to be praised.

PROVERBS 31:30 ESV

Modesty

Lord, I want to be a girl who dresses modestly. I don't want to wear short shorts or shirts that don't cover me. Your Word says that I should be a reflection of You, and that's what I want to do, and not just in my clothing! I want to be modest in my speech—not making dirty jokes or using bad words. I want every area of my life to be pure and spotless, because that's what You are. So help me with all of this, Lord. It's tempting to want to dress and act like the girls around me. I want to be separate, different from the rest, but I know it won't be easy. That's why I'm counting on You, Father! Amen.

You are God's people, so don't let it be said that any of you are immoral or indecent or greedy.

EPHESIANS 5:3 CEV

The Beauty of Holiness

I'm learning what holiness is, Lord. It means I'm set apart, not like others. I'm different because I'm more like You than I am like them. You've asked me to live a spectacular life, one You will be proud of. I know I'll still mess up from time to time, but I want to do my best to stick close to You because I know that true holiness comes from You, not me. I'm holy because You're holy. Honestly? I could try all day long and still mess things up! I'm so glad You're the One making me holy, Lord. Thank You! Amen.

As obedient children, do not be conformed to the passions of your former ignorance, but as he who called you is holy, you also be holy in all your conduct, since it is written, "You shall be holy, for I am holy."

1 PETER 1:14–16 ESV

Different, Set Apart, Beautiful!

Sometimes it bugs me a little that I'm different from everyone else. I don't always watch the movies or TV shows they like because I know there's not-so-great stuff in them. I don't wear some of the same clothes because I'm trying to be modest. I don't use bad language because I'm trying to keep my thoughts and my heart pure. So I'm different. I stand out. I'm set apart. I know that's okay with You, God. In fact, it makes me beautiful in Your sight! You created me to stand out, not blend in. You love when I'm set apart from the world. I need Your help to stay on the right path as I get older, Lord. Always remind me that "different" isn't bad. Amen.

Since you have been raised to new life with Christ, set your sights on the realities of heaven, where Christ sits in the place of honor at God's right hand. Think about the things of heaven, not the things of earth.

COLOSSIANS 3:1–2 NLT

PEER PRESSURE

They're trying to get you to do the wrong thing again, aren't they? Some of those friends of yours are sneaky. They want to lead you astray. But you're a daughter of the King. You won't be fooled. Nope. You'll keep walking with Him. You won't give in to the pressure to follow the crowd.

Upside-Down World

Things are a little crazy out there, Lord. People are doing and saying things that are the opposite of what the Bible says. They're living upside-down lives! It's so confusing because people are telling me that bad stuff is good and good stuff is bad. Why are they trying to get me so mixed up? I know what Your Word says—we're supposed to live holy lives. I want to live right-side-up in an upside-down world, but it's not always easy or popular. Will You help me, Lord? Help me to be a right-side-up girl, no matter what my friends are doing. Thanks in advance. I'm definitely going to need Your help with this one, Lord! Amen.

Do all things without grumbling or disputing, that you may be blameless and innocent, children of God without blemish in the midst of a crooked and twisted generation, among whom you shine as lights in the world.

PHILIPPIANS 2:14–15 ESV

Social Media

I'll admit it, Lord—I'm addicted. I love to carry around a phone or tablet because I want to be like the cool kids. It's fun to play games, but it's also fun to stay in touch with others. I talk to my grandparents in another state or visit with people who've moved away. Social media can be a great thing, but it can also be a time-stealer. Help me not to get too attached to apps on my phone so that I have more free time to spend with people face-to-face. Communicating in person is so much more fun than texting or messaging anyway! Amen.

You used to be like people living in the dark, but now you are people of the light because you belong to the Lord. So act like people of the light and make your light shine. Be good and honest and truthful, as you try to please the Lord.

EPHESIANS 5:8–10 CEV

Role Model

I want to be a good role model, Lord. I want to be the kind of girl others look up to. When they see me, I want them to say, "She's different from the others. She doesn't do some of the things others do." I know there are younger kids watching my actions, and I don't want to lead them down the wrong path. So give me courage, Lord. Help me to stand strong, even if it means I'm different from the other girls I know. Help me set a good example, I pray. Amen.

For the Spirit God gave us does not make us timid, but gives us power, love and self-discipline.

2 TIMOTHY 1:7 NIV

Peer Pressure

Dear Lord, I need to talk to You about something. It's something kind of hard. There's stuff going on at school and in my neighborhood. Kids are doing things they shouldn't. And they're trying to talk me into doing the wrong thing too. I don't want to go along with them—I really don't—but sometimes they almost convince me. I know in my heart that it's a bad choice, but I don't want my friends to hate me or to kick me out of the group. Today I'm asking You to give me the courage to stand up to them and to be brave. I want to be strong enough to say no to the things that break Your heart. What You think about me is so much more important than what my friends think, Father. May I never forget that. Amen.

Live wisely among those who are not believers,
and make the most of every opportunity.

COLOSSIANS 4:5 NLT

Living Your Faith

I don't always live my faith, Lord. I know You see when I mess up. I tell others I'm a Christian, then I slip up. I lie. I gossip. I give in to peer pressure. I want to be a girl who lives out her faith, one who really is who she says she is. I'll need Your help, Father. Teach me how to be consistent, no matter what I'm going through. Even when others make me angry, show me how to love. When they say mean things about me, help me to respond with kindness. Make me the strongest "me" I can be—a girl who loves You and loves others with her whole heart. I praise You in advance for the work You're doing in my heart. Amen.

Above all else, you must live in a way that brings honor to the good news about Christ. Then, whether I visit you or not, I will hear that all of you think alike. I will know that you are working together and that you are struggling side by side to get others to believe the good news.

PHILIPPIANS 1:27 CEV

Fitting In

Sometimes I feel like a puzzle piece that doesn't fit, Lord. I get around the girls at school and they all seem to get along so well. They're like peas in a pod. And me? I feel like an outsider. Oh, I try to fit. I do my best to dress like them, talk like them, and act like they act. But it doesn't always work, and I sometimes feel bad I tried so hard. I know I don't have to work to fit in with You, God. You love me, no matter what. I don't have to pretend to be something (or someone) I'm not. With You, it's completely natural. We get along great! Next time I'm tempted to fit in with those around me, remind me that I shouldn't try so hard. You'll bring just the right people into my life, and I'll trust Your timing. Amen.

Wish good for those who harm you; wish them well and do not curse them. Be happy with those who are happy, and be sad with those who are sad.

ROMANS 12:14–15 NCV

Cliques

I don't like it when my friends leave others out, Lord. It doesn't feel good to have cliques (circles of friends who won't let others in). I know what it feels like to be on the outside, wishing others would include me. It's terrible to be left out because of how you look or because you're not popular. It stinks to be told you don't fit in. I don't want to be like that. Help me to be the kind of friend who includes everyone. I want to have big circles, large groups that include all sorts of people, even those who are very different from me. May I never be a gossip or an excluder. May I always love and welcome people, even those who are nothing like me. The more the merrier, Lord! Amen.

I beg you, brothers and sisters, by the name of our Lord Jesus Christ that all of you agree with each other and not be split into groups. I beg that you be completely joined together by having the same kind of thinking and the same purpose.

1 CORINTHIANS 1:10 NCV

Be Who You Say You Are

I'll admit it, Lord—I'm not always who I say I am. I tell others that I'm a Christian, that I love You, then I treat them badly. I get angry. I throw a fit. I want to have my own way. I bend to peer pressure and follow the crowd. That's not very Christ-like, I know. Today, please help me be exactly who I say I am. Show me how to treat others fairly, with the kind of love that You would show them. I want to be a reflection of You, Jesus, so help me to do what You would do and say what You would say. I want to be who I say I am, but I'll need You to guide me. Amen.

Nothing is covered up that will not be revealed,
or hidden that will not be known.

LUKE 12:2 ESV

Please God, Not Others

Lord, sometimes I care *way* too much what other people think, especially the girls in the group I hang out with. I wonder what they will think about my hair or my clothes. Sometimes I even change the way I talk so I'll fit in with them. In other words, I care too much about pleasing them. From now on, I don't want to worry about all that. I only want to please You. I'll talk the way You want me to talk, dress the way You want me to dress, and even hang out with the girls (and boys) that You say are okay to hang out with. In the end, when I'm in heaven with You, the only thing that will matter is whether I've pleased You, Lord. So that's what I plan to do! Amen.

For am I now seeking the approval of man, or of God? Or am I trying to please man? If I were still trying to please man, I would not be a servant of Christ.

GALATIANS 1:10 ESV

Mean Girls

They drive me nuts, Lord! Those mean girls are a pain. They make life so hard, not just for me but for other girls too. Why do they always act like they're better than others? Why do they seem to have it out for me? Lord, today I choose to forgive the mean girls. I release my resentment of them and trust You to do a work in them. Change them from the inside out. Where there is hatred, teach them to love. Where there is bitterness, give them peace. In other words, change their hearts, Lord. Show them that they can live good, happy lives without causing pain to others. Thank You in advance. Amen.

Don't take part in doing those worthless things that are done in the dark. Instead, show how wrong they are. It is disgusting even to talk about what is done in the dark.

EPHESIANS 5:11–12 CEV

Good Choices

Sometimes it's hard to know which way to go. Do you make this choice or that choice? Spend some time talking with God about the choices you're facing, and He'll be happy to show you which way to go!

Let's Start Over

I need a do-over, Lord. I really messed this one up. I said something—did something—I wish I could take back. Can I just begin again? I'm so glad the Bible says I can! *Whew!* I don't know where I'd be if You didn't give second chances. Show me the right steps to take to make things right whenever I mess up, Lord. Teach me to come to You and ask forgiveness, then make things right with the people I've hurt. I want to honor You, Lord, so show me how to turn things around in a hurry when I've made mistakes. I know I'm not the only one who messes up, but I want to be quick to fix things. . .with Your help. Amen.

Do not let any unwholesome talk come out of your mouths, but only what is helpful for building others up according to their needs, that it may benefit those who listen.

EPHESIANS 4:29 NIV

Self-Care

Lord, sometimes I'm so busy—dealing with homework, school, sports, family stuff—that I don't really take good care of myself. I eat too much junk food. I don't brush my teeth enough. I don't sleep long enough at night. I have to be reminded to take a bath. It's not that I'm lazy, Lord. I'm just busy! But help me to remember that you care about my health. You want me to grow up strong. That means I have to stop and pay attention to the little things, like eating healthy food and getting a good night's sleep. You loved me enough to create me in Your image, Lord. Now I will do my best to take care of this body You gave me. Amen.

None of us hate our own bodies. We provide for them and take good care of them, just as Christ does for the church.

EPHESIANS 5:29 CEV

Obedience

Lord, I don't know why everyone acts like *obey* is some sort of bad word. It's not! It's actually one of the best words ever! When I obey my parents, my teachers, or other trusted adults, things work out better. When I disobey, I always end up regretting it. I feel sick inside, because I know I've done something wrong, even if others don't know yet. I don't like that feeling, Jesus. I'd rather do the right thing and feel good about it than to have those icky feelings that go along with disobedience. From now on, when I'm tempted to do the wrong thing, or when I'm feeling stubborn, remind me that I will feel better in the end if I just obey. My parents are happy when they don't have to keep reminding me to do the right thing. And Your heart is happy when I live an obedient life. Now that's a great way to live! Amen.

Do everything without grumbling or arguing.

PHILIPPIANS 2:14 CEV

Self-Control

Self-control is hard, Lord! "Look, but don't touch!" "Stay away from the candy jar!" "Don't disobey!" There are so many times I want to dive in and get what I want, even when it's not good for me. But You are teaching me self-control. You're showing me that it's healthier to control my urges. The next time I don't get what I want, I won't throw a fit. I'll just submit to Your will, Father. You know what's best. You're always looking out for me, and I'm so grateful for that! Teach me how to control myself, please. I'll be better off in the long run. Amen.

But the fruit of the Spirit is love, joy, peace, forbearance, kindness, goodness, faithfulness, gentleness and self-control. Against such things there is no law.

GALATIANS 5:22–23 NIV

Honesty

Oh boy, this is a hard one, Lord. I always tell people I'm an honest person, but sometimes I'm tempted to tell little white lies. I think I won't hurt anyone if I bend the truth a little. So I tell the teacher I left my homework at home when really I didn't do it. I tell my mom that my sister is to blame for the broken vase when I'm the one who broke it. I stretch the truth when telling a friend a juicy piece of gossip. I don't mean to hurt anyone, Lord, but it happens. Please help me to be honest, no matter what. I know it won't be easy, but it's a better way to live, for sure! And thanks for always being honest with me. I'm grateful. Amen.

For, "Whoever would love life and see good days must keep their tongue from evil and their lips from deceitful speech."

1 PETER 3:10 NIV

Guard Your Tongue

Lord, it's not easy to hold my tongue. So many times, I want to get things off my chest, to speak my mind. I want my voice to be heard. Sometimes it doesn't feel fair that I don't have a chance to talk when I want to. I'm learning, though, that most times it's better to guard my tongue, not to lash out when I'm angry or anxious. It's tough to keep my mouth closed! I'm so tempted to say the wrong thing or to speak in anger! I have to work extra hard not to say things I want to say. But with Your help, I can control myself. Instead of telling others, I'll tell You, Jesus. You're the best One to solve these problems anyway. Thanks for Your help with this, Lord. Amen.

Do not be quick with your mouth, do not be hasty in your heart to utter anything before God. God is in heaven and you are on earth, so let your words be few.

ECCLESIASTES 5:2 NIV

Forgiveness

Ugh! Sometimes I get really mad when people hurt my feelings or say bad things about me, Lord. I don't want to forgive them. I wonder why I should have to. They're the ones who were in the wrong after all. But Your Word says I need to forgive, even when it's really, really hard. So today I ask for Your help. I can't forgive unless You give me the power to do so. Help me to forgive those who've hurt me and then let go of any pain or bitterness. I want to walk in freedom, Lord, so show me how to release those who've wronged me. Heal those relationships, I pray, and teach me how to live in love. Amen.

Make allowance for each other's faults, and forgive anyone who offends you. Remember, the Lord forgave you, so you must forgive others.

COLOSSIANS 3:13 NLT

Healthy Eating

I'll admit it, Lord—I like junk food. Potato chips. Ice cream. French fries. Snowcones. Brownies with hot fudge sauce on top. . .*yum!* I could eat that stuff all day long. But I won't, because I've learned the hard way that too much of a good thing isn't really good. In fact, too much sugar can make me sick. So next time I'm tempted to drink too much soda or eat too much candy, remind me that there are healthier choices. Give me a love for veggies and fruits, Father, so that I can grow big and strong—healthy from the inside out. Amen.

Apply your heart to discipline and
your ears to words of knowledge.

PROVERBS 23:12 NASB

Cleanliness

Okay, confession time, Lord. I know You see into the messy spots—my closet, under my bed, the bathroom. You know when I let dirty clothes pile up or dust bunnies gather. You see when I leave dirty dishes in the sink or icky sticky cups filled with juice. You know when I forget to brush my teeth or wash my hair. You want me to live a clean life—my body, my clothes, and my surroundings. But I need Your help, Father! It doesn't come naturally to me. So give me a plan to keep my stuff clean and organized. Remind me when it's time to bathe or floss my teeth. I don't want to be a smelly girl. . .I want to be a smiley girl! Time to clean up my act, Lord. Amen.

"Wash yourselves; make yourselves clean; remove the evil of your deeds from before my eyes; cease to do evil."

ISAIAH 1:16 ESV

Exercise

I want to stay in good shape, Lord, so I need to exercise more. Can You give me ideas? I want to do things that will be fun—playing sports, swimming, playing games with my friends. And while I'm working on my physical body, help me to exercise my mind too. I want to stay active and alert so that the enemy doesn't tempt me to do the wrong things. May I be strong in body, mind, and soul, Father. That way I can be all You've created me to be. Amen.

For while bodily training is of some value, godliness is of value in every way, as it holds promise for the present life and also for the life to come.

1 TIMOTHY 4:8 ESV

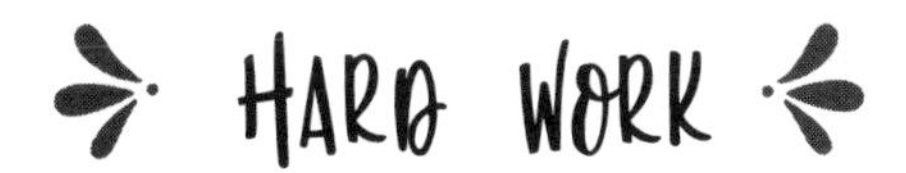

HARD WORK

Whew! You're tired. Between school, chores, sports, church, and other activities, you're ready for a nap. It's not time to give up yet! God has big things for you to do, and it's going to require hard work on your part. Are you ready for it? Let's go!

My Best

Sometimes I feel a little lazy, Lord. I don't want to get out of bed. I don't feel like cleaning my room. I don't want to go to school. It's more fun just to lie around and play video games or hang out with my friends. But I know that working hard is part of Your plan. You are the hardest worker of all! You made the whole world and everything in it. That must've been exhausting! I want to be like You, so I'll work hard too. Give me the energy to get the job done, no matter what. Dirty dishes? No problem! A messy closet? I'll clean it up! Hungry dog that needs fed? I'm on it! Whatever tasks I'm given, I'll do my best to work hard with a smile on my face. Thank You for the chance to be more like You, Father. Amen.

Do not be lazy but work hard, serving the Lord with all your heart.

ROMANS 12:11 NCV

Finding Your Calling

I wonder what I'm going to be when I grow up, Lord. I think about it all the time. Will I be a teacher? A doctor? A mom? A missionary? Will I travel around the world, exploring all sorts of amazing places I've never been before? Will I work on a computer in an office or in a laboratory as a scientist? Will I be a nurse, caring for little children, or will I work as a plumber, unclogging sinks? Only You know, and You're not telling! I know it's going to be a lot of work, but it's so exciting to think about the possibilities. I have so many creative ideas. I choose to trust in You, Lord. I submit myself to Your will for my life. I know You have great things in store for me, and I'm so grateful! Amen.

But the LORD said to me, "Do not say, 'I am too young.' You must go to everyone I send you to and say whatever I command you."

JEREMIAH 1:7 NIV

Things to Do

Whew! I've got so many things to do, Lord! My calendar is full to the brim. I've got school stuff, sports, church activities, family get-togethers, and so much more. I've got family vacations, homework, pets to take care of. I've got slumber parties, a messy bedroom to clean, and friends to hang out with. Sometimes I wonder how I'll keep it all in balance. But You'll show me. You have great things for me to do, and I know You'll help with the details. Most of all, show me how to keep things in the right order. Priorities, priorities! Make sure I deal with the most important stuff first, I pray. Amen.

"What you decide on will be done,
and light will shine on your ways."

JOB 22:28 NIV

Faithful in the Little Things

I'm always asking You to use me in big ways, Lord. I want to do great things for You! But sometimes I forget that You're testing me in the little tasks before giving me big stuff to do. You're watching to see how I do with things like keeping my room clean or staying on top of homework or loving my siblings. I want to pass the test! I want You to know that You can trust me to make a real difference in people's lives one day. Show me how to be faithful in the little things, Lord, so that one day great big opportunities will come my way. Amen.

"One who is faithful in a very little is also faithful in much, and one who is dishonest in a very little is also dishonest in much."

LUKE 16:10 ESV

The Wise Girl

I know there's a difference between being smart and being wise, Lord. I can get smarter and smarter by studying, but wisdom (real wisdom) comes from spending time with You. If I want to learn how to make good decisions, how to treat others kindly, or how to live a godly life, then I need to hang out with You. You'll give me wisdom to know right from wrong, to make excellent choices, and to be the best me I can be. Amen.

If any of you lacks wisdom, let him ask God, who gives generously to all without reproach, and it will be given him.

JAMES 1:5 ESV

Your Best Self

I don't always give my best, Lord. Sometimes I do things halfheartedly. I don't put all of my energy into some things, especially things like tidying up the living room or helping with the dishes or laundry. I just don't seem to care about those things as much. Help me to care, Lord. I want to give my all, no matter what I'm doing—in school, at church, at home, even when I'm alone in my bedroom. Show me how to take care of the things that matter, and help me to care more so that I can be my best possible self. I want to care like You care. Amen.

Do not be conformed to this world, but be transformed by the renewal of your mind, that by testing you may discern what is the will of God, what is good and acceptable and perfect.

ROMANS 12:2 ESV

Good Grades

I might not be like Einstein, Lord. I'm not a supersonic student, one who gets every answer right on the test. But I try my best! I want to get good marks in school, not just because my parents think it's important, but because I know good grades will help me one day get into a good college and eventually get a great job. I'll admit it—I need to pay more attention to my studies and less time playing. I need to focus on my homework and not on the TV or tablet or phone. In short, I need to buckle down. Help me do my very best work, Lord. I want to shine like an academic superstar, with Your help. Amen.

Make every effort to add to your faith goodness; and to goodness, knowledge.

2 PETER 1:5 NIV

Finish What You Start

It's not always easy to finish what I start, Lord. I'm terrific at starting—art projects, school assignments, organizing my closet, and so on. But sometimes I get bored and don't feel like finishing. I give up before the job is done. How come I have so much energy when I start, but I give up so quickly? Do I get bored, or what? I need Your help to finish, Father! I want to be known as a girl who finishes well. It's pointless to start well and fizzle out after all! So give me strength to get the job done, Lord. . .the *whole* job. I'll definitely need Your help with this. Amen.

I press on to reach the end of the race and receive the heavenly prize for which God, through Christ Jesus, is calling us.

PHILIPPIANS 3:14 NLT

School Woes

Some school days are harder than others, Lord. Things go wrong. I get in trouble for talking too much, I forget to do my homework, or I get a bad grade on a test. I struggle to learn, I end up getting in an argument with a friend, or I don't know the answer when the teacher calls on me. How embarrassing! Those days stink! I wish every school day could be perfect, but I know that's not going to happen, so I ask You to give me Your peace and courage on the hard days. Most of all, show me how to be a reflection of You during the hours I'm at school. I want to shine like a star, even on bad days. Amen.

Don't get angry. Don't be upset; it only leads to trouble.

PSALM 37:8 NCV

Athletics

Everywhere I turn, there are sports! Softball. Soccer. Gymnastics. Ballet. I could try so many different things! Today I want to thank You for athletics, Lord. It's a great way to stay healthy and have fun at the same time. And when I'm on a sports team, I have lots of new friends. We do fun things together—on the field and off. Help me choose wisely, Lord. Will I be a gymnast? A ballerina? A ballplayer? Will I stick with it for years or just take lessons for a while? I don't really know at this point, but I'm having fun figuring it out! Thanks for all the opportunities. Amen.

An athlete is not crowned unless he competes according to the rules.

2 TIMOTHY 2:5 ESV

SALVATION IN JESUS

The most important prayer you will ever pray is the one where you ask Jesus to come and live inside your heart, to be the King of your life. Have you done that yet? If not, today's the perfect day. Ask Him to forgive you for your sins, then watch as He washes away your past and leaves you white as snow!

Whiter Than Snow

I've been trying to figure this out, Lord. I mess up so many times, and not in small ways. I have big-time mess-ups. And yet the Bible says that I can be whiter than snow, that all my sins can be erased. Sometimes I try really, really hard not to mess up, but I don't have enough power to do it on my own. That's why I need You! I know I can't wash away my own sins. Only Jesus can do that. So I come to You, Lord—again and again—because You're so merciful and forgiving. You forgive me and wash me clean then say, *"It's okay! Start over!"* Thanks for making me white as snow, Lord. Amen.

"Come now, let us reason together, says the LORD: though your sins are like scarlet, they shall be as white as snow; though they are red like crimson, they shall become like wool."

ISAIAH 1:18 ESV

Jesus, My Savior

You came to save me, Jesus! You left heaven, that awesome, perfect place, and came all the way to earth as a baby, so that You could live a sinless life and then die on the cross, just for me. If I was the only person on earth, You still would have come. That's so amazing! You didn't want to miss one minute with me, so You made sure I received Your free gift of salvation. Now I'll get to live in heaven with You—*forever*! You saved me from my sin, my selfishness, and my bad habits. What a wonderful Savior You are, Jesus. I'm so thankful that You changed my life. Amen.

Jesus said to him, "I am the way, and the truth, and the life. No one comes to the Father except through me."

JOHN 14:6 ESV

Repentance

I don't always do the right thing, Lord. I know You know this. You see everything, even down into my heart. You know when I'm tempted to do the wrong thing. But You're a loving, gracious Father! You make me want to do right. So today I choose to turn away from the bad things I've done. I'll point myself in a different direction. Please forgive me for the things I've done that have hurt others. I know I've broken Your heart at times. I want to live a godly life filled with possibilities. So I repent and turn back to You, Father. Thanks for welcoming me back, even after I've made mistakes. Amen.

The Lord is not slow to fulfill his promise as some count slowness, but is patient toward you, not wishing that any should perish, but that all should reach repentance.

2 PETER 3:9 ESV

The Words in Red

I love Your Word, Lord! The Bible is filled with great advice for how to live my life. I especially love the words that, in many Bibles, are marked in red, the words of Jesus. When I read the red words, I know they're extra powerful, because Jesus spoke them out loud to His disciples, His followers, and to me! It's crazy-cool to think that He knew I would one day be alive! I can almost hear His voice now, as I read the words. They leap off the page! He's telling me to live a life that is pleasing to Him, to walk close to Him always, and to love others the way I want to be loved. No matter how many books I read, there will never be words more important than the ones in red. I promise to keep them close to my heart. Amen.

"If you abide in me, and my words abide in you, ask whatever you wish, and it will be done for you."

JOHN 15:7 ESV

The Great Love of Jesus

Jesus, Your love is deeper than any ocean. It reaches all the way down to the bottom when I'm hurting. It's higher than any mountain. It shines like a beacon that can be seen for miles away. It's more tender than a baby's skin, tougher than an athlete's muscles, and it's able to work miracles, touching even the hardest heart. Your love means everything to me, Lord. It picks me up when I'm down, encourages me when I'm depressed, and makes me want to sing a song of praise. Thank You for loving me, even when I make mistakes. You're so kind to me even when I mess up. From the bottom of my heart, I thank You for Your amazing love. Amen!

But God shows his great love for us in this way:
Christ died for us while we were still sinners.

ROMANS 5:8 NCV

Jesus First

You know every answer to every question, Lord! When I put You first in my life—above my friends, sports, electronics, schoolwork, and family—everything else always works out. I'm not saying I always get it right. Sometimes things get out of order. I forget to put You first. Things go wrong and I wonder why. Instead of going to You, asking for Your help, I try to fix things myself. Sometimes I just get panicked and think everything is falling apart. Then I remember. . .everything works better when the Boss is in charge. So today, I submit to You. I don't want to be the boss of my life. Take Your place at the top, Lord, and I know everything will work out exactly as You have planned. Amen.

Jesus said to him, "I am the way, and the truth, and the life. No one comes to the Father except through me."

JOHN 14:6 ESV

Following Jesus

Sometimes I'm a follower, Lord. I see girls in a group and I want to be part of it, so I do what they do. I dress like they dress. I talk like they talk. I make fun of the girls they make fun of. You don't want me to follow after people. I know that. But You do want me to follow You. So today, I choose to love as You love, to serve as You serve, to act as You act. I want to be a Jesus-follower all the way! I know that means I have to change a few things—like my attitude and my desire to be like others—but that's okay! I really do want to be like You, Jesus, so lead me wherever You want me to go! Amen.

Then [Jesus] said to the crowd, "If any of you wants to be my follower, you must give up your own way, take up your cross daily, and follow me. If you try to hang on to your life, you will lose it. But if you give up your life for my sake, you will save it."

LUKE 9:23–24 NLT

The Shame Game

Sometimes I feel so ashamed, Lord. I do something wrong in complete secret then feel ashamed of myself. So I confess and make things right again. I should feel better after getting my wrongdoing off my chest, but I still feel ashamed every time I think about it. I try not to think about it, but then I feel ashamed all over again. It's time for that shame to go, in Jesus' name! I know a little conviction is a good thing, but You always forgive me and wash away my shame. You don't want me to wallow in it. You want me to start over with a smile on my face, ready to do better next time. So thanks for taking away my shame, Lord. I'm so happy to be done with it. Amen.

But the Lord GOD helps me; therefore I have not been disgraced; therefore I have set my face like a flint, and I know that I shall not be put to shame.

ISAIAH 50:7 ESV

Salvation

Lord, I'm finally figuring out what it means to be saved. Jesus left heaven and came to earth. He died on the cross and gave His life in place of mine. If I accept His free gift of salvation, I can live forever in heaven. Wow! What a trade-off! My sinful life in exchange for Jesus' perfect life? Of course I'm saying *yes* to that! It would be silly *not* to! I can't wait to share the Good News with others so they can receive Your salvation too. I can't wait to see all the people in heaven who have said yes to Jesus. How fun that will be! Thanks for saving me, Lord. Amen.

For the wages of sin is death, but the free gift of God is eternal life in Christ Jesus our Lord.

ROMANS 6:23 ESV

Jesus

I hear people talking about Your Son, Jesus, all the time, Lord. Some people say He was a great man. Other people say He was a prophet. But I love what Your Word says: He was—and is—Your Son, and He did something no one else has ever done. He came to earth, knowing He would have to die on a cross. He chose to give up His life so that others could live. Who does that?! Jesus lived an amazing, sinless life. He healed people and taught them how to live. There will never be anyone else like Jesus. Today I choose to praise Him at the top of my lungs! Amen.

For God so loved the world that he gave his one and only Son, that whoever believes in him shall not perish but have eternal life.

JOHN 3:16 NIV

GROWING UP

First you want it to happen fast; then you want it to slow down. Growing up ain't for sissies! So many changes are happening in your heart, your mind, and your body. But don't worry. God already knows where these changes will lead you. It's going to be so much fun to watch it all happen!

Changes

Every day I look in the mirror and see changes, Lord! I'm growing. My parents keep having to buy me new clothes! Even my feet are changing. I've gone through a lot of shoes since I was a baby! I know that growing up is part of Your plan for me. Sometimes I like to imagine what I'll look like when I'm a teenager or a grown-up. Will I have my mom's hair? Will I have my dad's big feet? It's hard to know, but I'm excited to find out. So I've decided to enjoy the changes, Lord. Thanks for showing me the reflection in the mirror. It's fun to watch myself grow up! Amen.

And now, just as you accepted Christ Jesus as your Lord, you must continue to follow him. Let your roots grow down into him, and let your lives be built on him. Then your faith will grow strong in the truth you were taught, and you will overflow with thankfulness.

COLOSSIANS 2:6–7 NLT

Enjoying Childhood

It's great to be a kid, Lord! I don't have to worry about paying bills or having a job. Sure, I have to go to school, but that's kind of fun anyway. Being a kid means I get to play with friends, go swimming at the pool, learn cool new stuff, discover my talents, and spend lots of time with my family. I'm not in a big hurry to be a teenager, Lord. It's kind of cool to be young and carefree, to not have to worry about stuff like money problems or dating. I know things will change as I get older, but for now I plan to just go on being a kid and enjoying life. Amen.

Don't let anyone look down on you because you are young, but set an example for the believers in speech, in conduct, in love, in faith and in purity.

1 TIMOTHY 4:12 NIV

Crushes

A lot of the girls are doing it, Lord. . .they're giggling and talking about which boys they like. They have crushes on this one or that one. They talk about how cute the boy with the blond hair is or how sweet and funny the one with black hair is. I try not to get caught up in those conversations, Lord, but it's hard. Before long, I find myself talking about boys too. I know I'm too young for any serious boy-girl relationships, so help me. Guard my thoughts. Keep me pure. When the time is right, You'll show me. Until then, protect my heart, I pray. Amen.

Walk with the wise and become wise,
for a companion of fools suffers harm.

PROVERBS 13:20 NIV

Physical Changes

Lord, can I talk to You about something kind of awkward? My body is going through changes—and some of them are kind of weird—but I know that You designed my body, so I figure You're the best One to talk to about this. Am I going to change. . .a lot? Is it going to hurt? Will I feel strange? Are other girls going through the same changes? I know the Bible says You'll be with me every step of the way, so I choose to trust in You, no matter how much things change. You knew this was coming, Lord, and You even know what I'm going to look like on the other side of it. I wish I knew, but I guess I'll see soon enough. Help me through this process of change, please! Amen.

Therefore we do not lose heart. Though outwardly we are wasting away, yet inwardly we are being renewed day by day. For our light and momentary troubles are achieving for us an eternal glory that far outweighs them all. So we fix our eyes not on what is seen, but on what is unseen, since what is seen is temporary, but what is unseen is eternal.

2 CORINTHIANS 4:16–18 NIV

Boys

Ugh! Sometimes boys drive me crazy. They're so. . .different. I don't get them at all. Then, other times, I feel a little jealous. Boys seem to have it easier in many ways. They don't have to worry about how they wear their hair or how stylish their clothes are. They don't gossip about one another as much as girls do. At least it doesn't seem that way. Some of my friends are really starting to like boys, Lord. They have crushes. I'm glad I don't have to worry about that for a while. I can be friends with a boy, but crushing on him can wait! In the meantime, help me have good relationships with the boys—brothers, cousins, friends, classmates—in my life. Amen.

So God created man in his own image, in the image of God he created him; male and female he created them.

GENESIS 1:27 ESV

Growing Up Too Fast

Lord, sometimes I feel like I'm growing up *way* too fast. I want to be like the older girls, to have the cool clothes, hair, and makeup. I want to look and act older than I am. I want to watch TV shows that the big kids watch and go to the mall with my friends, no parents allowed! But You're not in a big hurry for me to change. In fact, You have all sorts of things to teach me while I'm still young. So I'll stop trying to rush things. I'll settle in and be a kid for a while. I'll even let Mom tag along to the mall. She's kind of cool anyway. There will be plenty of time to be grown up later. For now, I'll go on being a kid. Amen.

Jesus said, "Let the little children come to me, and do not hinder them, for the kingdom of heaven belongs to such as these."

MATTHEW 19:14 NIV

A Lifelong Journey

Lord, I've been thinking about what my life will be like when I'm older. I don't know who I'll marry or how many kids I'll have, but I do know one thing: I will always be Your daughter. I'll always walk hand in hand with You. I'll never stop loving You, Lord. That's a promise. I know I can trust You, not just now, but for all of my life. So why would I ever stop hanging out with You? I won't stop! This is going to be an amazing journey, and I plan to walk next to You every step of the way. Thanks for guiding me, Lord! Amen.

Now make me completely happy! Live in harmony by showing love for each other. Be united in what you think, as if you were only one person.

PHILIPPIANS 2:2 CEV

Creativity

You're such a creative heavenly Father! You made all things—long-necked giraffes, squishy-faced pug dogs, hysterical hyenas, even precious newborn puppies and kittens. I adore Your creation. I love the beautiful sunsets, the sound of the ocean waves, the mountains covered in snow, and the autumn leaves turning red and gold. What an imagination You have, Lord! Now I know why I'm so imaginative. I'm created in Your image. I also want to create masterpieces in my own special way. I have a feeling You're going to show me how to do that as I get older. I can't wait to see how creative I will become. Thanks for making me like You! Amen.

"He has filled him with the Spirit of God,
with skill, with intelligence, with knowledge,
and with all craftsmanship, to devise artistic
designs, to work in gold and silver and bronze."

EXODUS 35:31–32 ESV

Prince Charming

All the girls are talking about him, Lord: Prince Charming. They think he's going to come riding in on a white horse and sweep them away to their very own happily-ever-after. I'm not sure if I believe all that, but I do secretly hope that one day I'll have my own prince. Whether it happens or not, I already have the best One! Your Word says that Jesus is the ultimate Prince Charming. He's coming on a white horse someday. Wow! I know that my life will have a good ending because I've put my trust in Jesus as my Savior. Once upon a time, I'll get to live in a mansion in heaven. Talk about a true happily-ever-after! Amen.

Now I saw heaven opened, and behold, a white horse. And He who sat on him was called Faithful and True, and in righteousness He judges and makes war. His eyes were like a flame of fire, and on His head were many crowns. He had a name written that no one knew except Himself.

REVELATION 19:11–12 NKJV

Spiritual Growth

My body is growing and changing so much, Lord! Sometimes I look at pictures from a year or two ago, and I hardly recognize the girl staring back at me. She looks totally different now. But I'm not just changing on the outside. I'm changing on the inside too, Lord. As I read my Bible and pray, I'm growing, growing, growing on the inside. I'm becoming a stronger Christian. My faith is growing. It's not always easy, but I'm learning so much. I trust You to "grow me" into the woman of God You want me to be. What an exciting journey! Amen.

Finally, let the mighty strength of the Lord make you strong. Put on all the armor that God gives, so you can defend yourself against the devil's tricks.

EPHESIANS 6:10–11 CEV

You don't like going through hard times. No one does. But the Bible doesn't promise a carefree life. Bad stuff happens, but God is still in control. He won't leave you or forsake you. Best of all, He cares about all the things you care about. He's got this. Don't panic.

Love the Unlovable

Not everyone is easy to love, Lord. There are some people who make it difficult. Some of the people I know are rude to others or talk bad about people behind their backs. Can I be really honest and say these people get on my nerves? I know Your Word says I should love everyone, but I don't always *want* to love these meanies. I want to give them a piece of my mind. But I won't. Can You help me to see them the way that You see them? I want to love them the way You do, Father. And who knows? Maybe one day some of these hard-to-love people will become my good friends. It could happen! Anything is possible when love leads the way. Amen.

Beloved, if God so loved us, we also ought to love one another.

1 JOHN 4:11 ESV

Hard Times

So many people are going through hard times, Lord. It breaks my heart. Some of them are struggling to pay the bills. Others are going through a health crisis. Some of my friends have even had their parents get divorced. It's so sad, all of it. I've gone through hard times too, but I know You're already there for me. Even when I'm crying—when my heart is completely broken—You're there. When I'm confused or upset, You promise never to leave me. Today I ask You to bring comfort to friends and family members who are going through a tough season, Lord. Hold them close, I pray. Amen.

No temptation has overtaken you that is not common to man. God is faithful, and he will not let you be tempted beyond your ability, but with the temptation he will also provide the way of escape, that you may be able to endure it.

1 CORINTHIANS 10:13 ESV

Abuse

Sometimes I hear stories about people being hurt, Lord. Like that time I found out one of my friends was getting beat up by her older sister, or that other time when I found out my brother was being picked on by kids at school. It breaks my heart to see others getting hurt, and I never know what to do. Should I tell someone? Should I let my teacher know that the boy next to me is calling me bad names? Should I tell my mom that the girl who lives down the street is crying because of something bad her grandpa did to her? Give me the courage to speak up, Lord! I don't like to be a tattletale, but letting others know about abuse is always right. Help me, I pray. May I never stay silent when abuse is taking place! Amen.

The LORD tests the righteous, but his soul hates the wicked and the one who loves violence.

PSALM 11:5 ESV

Gossip

Gossip is a terrible thing, Lord. I know what it's like to be the girl everyone else is talking about. It hurts. . .a lot. I also know what it's like to talk about others. I don't really do it on purpose, but sometimes I get caught up in conversations and before you know it—*bam!*—I'm gossiping. I don't want to be like this. Can You help me? Next time I start to gossip, put a clamp on my tongue. Stop me from saying bad things. Don't let me join in—laughing at someone behind her back just because she's different or made a mistake. Help me remember that You love everyone just the same. I want to be a good example for others, Lord, and I need Your help! Amen.

Don't let anyone trick you with foolish talk. God punishes everyone who disobeys him and says foolish things. So don't have anything to do with anyone like that.

EPHESIANS 5:6–7 CEV

Hurt Feelings

It doesn't feel good when people make fun of me, Lord. It hurts my feelings. Sometimes they're joking around. I get that. But that doesn't make it hurt any less. When people say rude things about my hair, my skin, my teeth, my clothes, or my house. . .it really bothers me. When they comment on my grades or my habits, it stings. Help me forgive those people. And may I never be like that! I don't ever want to be the sort of person who makes fun of others or deliberately hurts them. When I see someone struggling to fit in, help me be a friend to the friendless. May everyone know that I'm a girl who cares. Amen.

"But I say to you, Love your enemies and pray for those who persecute you."

MATTHEW 5:44 ESV

Praying for Your Enemies

I don't like having enemies, Lord. In fact, I never thought I would have any. But some of the people I thought I could trust—my friends—have turned out to be enemies. I call them "frenemies," because they still pretend to be my friend some of the time. Today I choose to pray for those who have hurt me. I forgive the ones who've done bad things to me or spoken mean words. Even if we never become true friends, I pray that the bitterness will end. Show us how to treat one another kindly. I know You prayed for Your enemies, Jesus. If You could do it—especially after how they treated You—then I can too! Amen.

Let love be your guide. Christ loved us and offered his life for us as a sacrifice that pleases God.

EPHESIANS 5:2 CEV

Prejudice

I don't like the word *prejudice*, Lord. It makes me sad when people judge others because of the color of their skin or because they dress or look different. To judge someone on outward appearance is wrong. I know that You love all people, no matter what. I want to be like You. If I'm ever tempted to treat someone differently, please check my heart and show me a better way. Help me to love the way You love and to serve the way You serve. I don't want to judge others, Father. I want to love them as You do, no matter how different from me they might be. Amen.

There is neither Jew nor Gentile, neither slave nor free, nor is there male and female, for you are all one in Christ Jesus.

GALATIANS 3:28 NIV

Death

I don't like to think about death, Lord. I know that heaven is a wonderful place, but I still feel really sad when I think about people dying. I will miss them so much! Help me not to be afraid of death, Father. Whenever I get sad thinking about it, remind me that one day I will get to see my friends and family members again in heaven. There, in that wonderful place, there will be no more pain, no more crying, nothing but pure bliss! Thank You for creating a place for us to go where nothing bad ever happens. When I'm reminded of what heaven is like, all of my sadness goes away. Thanks for that, Lord. Amen.

For since we believe that Jesus died and rose again, even so, through Jesus, God will bring with him those who have fallen asleep.

1 THESSALONIANS 4:14 ESV

Disagreements

I don't like to disagree with people, Lord, but it happens. I get into an argument with my sister. I fight with my best friend. I even get mad at my mom. When I disagree, it means I'm out of agreement with that person. Being out of agreement is tough, no matter who it is. But You're the great solver of all problems, Lord. You can mend our disagreements and help us stay close. No, I won't always agree with others. But that doesn't mean we can't be friends. With Your help, my relationships with others can grow stronger, in spite of our differences. Thanks for showing me that. Amen.

Be brave when you face your enemies. Your courage will show them that they are going to be destroyed, and it will show you that you will be saved. God will make all of this happen.

PHILIPPIANS 1:28 CEV

Loneliness

I know what it's like to feel lonely, Lord. I've felt that way at times, even when people were with me. Sometimes I feel invisible, like people don't even see me. I try to get their attention, but they don't always notice me. So I stop trying. I give up and stick to myself. Then I get even lonelier. I know the best way to have a friend is to be a friend, so from now on I'm going to try harder to make others feel included. That way neither one of us will be lonely anymore. We'll have each other. Thank You for putting other people in my life, people who can be my friends, my family, my circle. Amen.

God sets the lonely in families, he leads out the prisoners with singing; but the rebellious live in a sun-scorched land.

PSALM 68:6 NIV

Joy and Thanksgiving

Have you ever met someone who's always bubbly? Are you that sort of person? God loves it when you have a cheerful heart, even when you're going through hard times. If you ask Him to give you His deep-down joy, He'll do it.

Joy

I'm a bubbly kind of girl, Lord! I get the giggles. I laugh. I tell jokes. I like to make my friends smile, especially when they're going through hard stuff. When other people around me are gloomy and sad, I do my best to cheer them up. I know that joy comes from You. You make tough days better. You give me joy even when I'm going through hard stuff. I don't have to pretend to be happy. You give me *real* joy—the kind that comes from deep down in my heart. I'm so grateful You've placed bubbling joy in my heart, Father! May I spread it to everyone I see today! Amen.

Always be joyful. Never stop praying. Be thankful in all circumstances, for this is God's will for you who belong to Christ Jesus.

1 THESSALONIANS 5:16–18 NLT

Thankfulness

Sometimes I forget to thank You, Lord—for the beautiful weather, the blue skies, my family, my house, my friends, even my pets. I forget that You're the One who has given me everything—my clothes, my shoes, my bed, even my toys. You've given me good health, great food to eat, and even a terrific imagination. Today I choose to say, "Thank You so much for all You've done for me!" You've kept me safe, given me a family to live with, and provided for my every need. You're such a generous heavenly Father, and I'm so grateful that You love me enough to make sure I have everything I need in life. Thank You, Lord! Amen.

Let the peace of Christ rule in your hearts, to which indeed you were called in one body; and be thankful.

COLOSSIANS 3:15 NASB

Enjoy Yourself!

I'm so glad that You think it's okay to have fun, Lord. In fact, You invented fun! You want me to enjoy myself. So today I choose to do just that. I plan to have a blast everywhere I go. I want to make people laugh and smile. I want to bring joy even to hard situations. Show me how to love others the way You do so that I can bring hope, Father. And while You're at it, help others around me learn how to enjoy life too. Some of them are pretty stressed out. Give them supernatural joy to see beyond their problems to the great things You are doing in their lives. Thanks for such a wonderful life, Lord. Amen.

There is nothing better for a person than that he should eat and drink and find enjoyment in his toil. This also, I saw, is from the hand of God, for apart from him who can eat or who can have enjoyment?

ECCLESIASTES 2:24–25 ESV

Laughter

I can't help it, Lord! Sometimes I just get the giggles. I start laughing and can't stop. People look at me funny, but what can I do? Once it gets going, it's contagious. Before long, others are laughing too. That's when things really get crazy! I love that the Bible says laughter is like a medicine. It's true! Laughter makes me feel better, especially when I've been having a rough day. It hits the spot! So go ahead, Lord. Give me the giggles. I can take it, especially on the hard days when things aren't going my way. A little laughter will cure whatever ails me. Thanks for such fun medicine, Lord. Amen.

Then our mouth was filled with laughter, and our tongue with shouts of joy; then they said among the nations, "The LORD has done great things for them."

PSALM 126:2 ESV

Gratitude

I don't always remember to tell my mom or dad how grateful I am for all they do for me, Lord. And I often forget to thank all the people who serve me every day—the lunch worker at school, the school bus driver, the clerk at the grocery store. These people all work hard to make my life easier, and I really am thankful. I want to be a girl who lets others know she's grateful for their acts of service. I know how good it feels when people show gratitude to me. So show me who to thank today, Lord. I want to get busy showing gratitude! Amen.

Give thanks in all circumstances; for this is the will of God in Christ Jesus for you.

1 THESSALONIANS 5:18 ESV

Thankful for Your Power

I know where my power to make good choices comes from, Lord. It comes from You! By myself, I'm a weakling! I have no spiritual muscles at all. But with Your help, I can do anything. When I go through hard stuff—and I know I will—I won't try to fix it myself. I'll trust in You instead. I'll plug into Your power source. And I'll tell other people to do the same thing. I'll share the message that real power comes from above. Thank You for being my Helper, Lord. I'm so thankful for Your power! Amen.

"When you pass through the waters, I will be with you; and when you pass through the rivers, they will not sweep over you. When you walk through the fire, you will not be burned; the flames will not set you ablaze."

ISAIAH 43:2 NIV

No Greed Here!

I don't want to be a greedy girl, Lord, one who always demands, demands, demands. How rude! I want to be a giving, generous girl, one who is known for her thankfulness, not her greed. May I always remember that it's more blessed to give than to receive. May I run from greed and be thankful for the things I already have! It doesn't matter how many toys I have or how many cool outfits are in my dresser drawers. All that matters is how I treat people. So I won't hog the best stuff. I won't demand my own way. I'll lay down my greed and make sure others get what they need first. Help me, I pray. Amen.

Then He said to them, "Beware, and be on your guard against every form of greed; for not even when one has an abundance does his life consist of his possessions."

LUKE 12:15 NASB

Joy in Troubled Times

I don't know how You do it, Lord, but You always seem to know when I'm down in the dumps. I can't hide my depression from You. You see everything, and You know just how to lift my spirits. In fact, You regularly turn my frown upside down. Before long, I'm all giggly and wiggly, filled with joy and laughter. That's what an amazing God You are! Today I want to thank You for giving me joy—in good times and bad—but especially during the hard times. I've got the "joy, joy, joy, joy down in my heart," and it's all because of You, Lord. Thank You so much! Amen.

We also have joy with our troubles, because we know that these troubles produce patience. And patience produces character, and character produces hope. And this hope will never disappoint us, because God has poured out his love to fill our hearts. He gave us his love through the Holy Spirit, whom God has given to us.

ROMANS 5:3–5 NCV

Not Just a Season

Sometimes people act like Thanksgiving is the only time of year they should be thankful, Lord! Truth is, we need to thank You all year long—when things are going well, and even when they aren't. So the next time I'm in a jam—struggling in school or bickering with a friend—remind me that I said that! I want to stop and thank You right then and there! There's power in giving thanks after all. Oh sure. . .I'll have plenty to talk about next Thanksgiving. But hopefully between now and then I'll stop and praise You hundreds, if not thousands, of times. I'll start right now: Thanks for an awesome day, Lord! You are worthy of my praise. Amen.

And let them offer sacrifices of thanksgiving,
and tell of his deeds in songs of joy!

PSALM 107:22 ESV

Down in My Heart

Lord, I don't like bad days. Is it okay to admit that? I really don't. When things go wrong, I forget that I'm supposed to be joyful. Then I'm reminded of that song, the one about having joy "down in my heart." That means there's a little seed of joy in my heart all the time, in good times and bad. If I want it to grow and blossom, I have to water it—make use of it—even on the bad days. So let it grow, Lord! I'll praise You no matter what, even if it's really, really hard. You are worthy of my praise regardless of what is going on in my life. Thank You for the reminder, Lord! Amen.

Let us come into his presence with thanksgiving; let us make a joyful noise to him with songs of praise!

PSALM 95:2 ESV

Did you realize that God gave you special gifts so that you could help others? It's true! Loving and serving others is part of God's plan for your life. Who is He asking you to serve? Which gifts will you use? It's going to be so fun to find out!

Missions

Lord, I know there are people living all over this big world who don't know You. Some of them live in countries far, far away. Others live nearby, in my own neighborhood. It's crazy to think that some of my own neighbors don't know You, Jesus, but it's true. How can I help, Lord? I can't be a missionary, not like the ones who come to my church anyway. I can't move away to Africa or Asia. Show me how to share my faith with people I pass by every day—the friend on the school bus, the woman who lives across the street, the boy who says mean things to me in class. I want to be a good witness for You, Jesus, but I'll definitely need Your help with this one. I want to "go into all the world" and share the good news that You love everyone. Amen.

And then [Jesus] told them, "Go into all the world and preach the Good News to everyone."

MARK 16:15 NLT

Volunteering

I love to volunteer, Lord, to give freely of my time and efforts to help others. Whether I'm working in the nursery at church or volunteering at a local food pantry, I have a blast helping others. Give me creative ideas, Father. Where do You want me to volunteer? At a homeless shelter? At a children's home? At a nursing home, visiting with the elderly? Maybe I could read books to children at the library. I'm excited about the possibilities. I'll go where You ask me to go, Lord—as long as Mom and Dad agree—and I'll share the love of Jesus with people I meet along the way. Thanks for showing me how to volunteer! Amen.

"In all things I have shown you that by working hard in this way we must help the weak and remember the words of the Lord Jesus, how he himself said, 'It is more blessed to give than to receive.'"

ACTS 20:35 ESV

Sacrifice

Lord, I have to admit, I don't always like to sacrifice, to give of myself for others. Sometimes I have to sacrifice my time helping Mom clean when I'd rather be playing. Other times I have to sacrifice my clothes or toys, sharing with my sister or a friend in need. There have even been times when I've had to sacrifice getting to do something fun with my family because of bad behavior on my part. If anyone understands sacrifice, it's You, Jesus. You sacrificed Your life on the cross so that I could live for all eternity. Wow! If You could do that for me, then surely I can sacrifice my time and energy for those around me. Help me, I pray. Amen.

If someone does wrong to you, do not pay him back by doing wrong to him. Try to do what everyone thinks is right.

ROMANS 12:17 NCV

Sensitivity

I'll admit it, Lord—sometimes I'm not paying attention to what others are going through. Maybe a friend is having a bad day or my mom has a headache. And I don't even notice. Or if I do, it doesn't really change my behavior. I want to be more sensitive to others, Lord. I want to be the sort of person who notices when others are hurting. May I be as sweet and loving to them as they are to me when I'm going through a hard time. Today, please show me someone I can pray for, someone who's going through a rough time. I want to be sensitive to their needs, Lord. Amen.

But a Samaritan, as he traveled, came where the man was; and when he saw him, he took pity on him.

LUKE 10:33 NIV

Random Acts of Kindness

I love surprising people, Lord! Sometimes, when my mom's really busy, I'll clean the kitchen or vacuum the living room for her. When my dad is working in the yard, I offer to help. When I see a girl at school who's having a hard time, I give her an encouraging card or a candy bar. I love going out of my way to surprise others with random acts of kindness. Today, give me creative ideas. Show me how I can bless others when they least expect it. I want to surprise people with my kindness, Lord, and I know You can show me how. Amen.

Do not let kindness and truth leave you; bind them around your neck, write them on the tablet of your heart.

PROVERBS 3:3 NASB

The Golden Rule

My idea of "do unto others" isn't always the same as Yours, Lord! Sometimes I want to get even. I want to embarrass or hurt others because I know they plan to do the same to me. But You want me to live a different sort of life. You want me to treat other people the way I *want* to be treated. That changes everything! I want to be treated as an equal. I want to be treated fairly. I want to be treated with love and grace. I want to be included. So I guess that means I have to treat others that way, even if it's hard. Today I'll do my best to show love and grace to people, because that's what I want them to do for me. It might not be easy, but I'll give it my best shot. . .with Your help. Amen.

"Do to others as you would have them do to you."

LUKE 6:31 NIV

Giving

You're such a generous Father! You give me everything I need—the clothes I'm wearing, food, a home, even friends and family. I want to be generous too! I want to be the kind of girl who sees what others need and tries to help. It's not always easy to give, I know. Sometimes I want to hang on to my stuff instead of giving it away. But You can help me with that. Show me who to help, and then give me creative ideas. Will I support a missionary in India? Will I support a child overseas? Can I help out with a local ministry or give to a food pantry? The opportunities are endless. Show me Your plan for my giving, Lord, and I'll gladly obey. Amen!

Now you should finish what you started. Let the eagerness you showed in the beginning be matched now by your giving. Give in proportion to what you have.

2 CORINTHIANS 8:11 NLT

Sharing the Gospel

I know You've asked me to shine my light, Lord, and I'm trying! In my school and my neighborhood. . .but it's not always easy. There are people who don't want to know about You. They just want me to act like them, to blend in. But I'm going to stand firm, Lord! I'll keep on trying even when they make it hard, because I know it's important to You and it's part of being a Christian. I want to be an example, not just to people my age but to the adults in my community too. Give me creative ideas so that I can shine Your light even brighter. I want everything I do to point to You, Lord. Amen.

"In the same way, let your light shine before others, so that they may see your good works and give glory to your Father who is in heaven."

MATTHEW 5:16 ESV

Generosity

I love generous people, Lord! They're beautiful from the inside out. These amazing people are always making sure I have what I need. Sometimes they surprise me with their generosity, giving me unexpected gifts or treats. I love when that happens. . .mostly because I love surprises! I want to be generous like that. I want to be the kind of person who gives when people least expect it. Show me how to give like You do, Lord, filled with surprises at every turn. I can't wait to see who we're going to surprise first. What fun this is going to be! Amen.

"Give, and it will be given to you. Good measure, pressed down, shaken together, running over, will be put into your lap. For with the measure you use it will be measured back to you."

LUKE 6:38 ESV

Serving Those with Disabilities

Father, today I'm thinking about my friends and acquaintances who have disabilities. They're amazing, Lord! Some are in wheelchairs, but that doesn't stop them! They're super-brave. They do all sorts of activities, even if it's hard. Others have disabilities that can't be seen, but they do amazing things too. The truth is, there are no limits, no matter what we're facing in this life. As long as we stick close to You, we can accomplish anything. So show me how I can help those who are struggling, I pray. Give them courage. Give them friends. Meet every need. And may I always see them as You do—as Your perfect, amazing kids. Amen.

This is my prayer for you: that your love will grow more and more; that you will have knowledge and understanding with your love.

PHILIPPIANS 1:9 NCV

BIG STUFF AHEAD!

God has big plans for you, girl. *Big* plans! And even though you can't see where the road leads, He can! He's going to take you on an amazing journey with Him. Just hold His hand tightly and pray every step of the way.

Goals

There are so many things I want to accomplish in my life, Jesus! I have big plans for myself. I can see it all now! I want to be an excellent student. I want to go to college. I want to play sports. I want to sing songs or act on the big stage. I want to have friends, go to parties, tell other people about Jesus. There are so many amazing things on my to-do list! I don't know where the road will take me or how many of my goals I'm going to accomplish, but with Your help I can do a lot more than I could ever do on my own. So today I choose to give my goals to You. Take me where You want me to go, Lord. I can't wait to see what the future holds! Amen.

So we keep on praying for you, asking our God to enable you to live a life worthy of his call. May he give you the power to accomplish all the good things your faith prompts you to do.

2 THESSALONIANS 1:11 NLT

God's Dreams for You

I've got so many cool ideas about what my life will be like when I'm grown up—what sort of job I'll do, who I'll marry, how many kids I'll have, what sort of house I'll live in. My dreams are huge! Then I remember that Your dreams and wishes for me are even bigger than my own. You have supernatural ideas! Wowza! I can hardly wait to see all that You have planned. Today I choose to lay down my wants and wishes and say, "Your will be done, Father!" because I know that anything I dream up is nothing in comparison to what You have in mind. Great things are ahead, supernatural things! I can feel it. Amen.

"For I know the plans I have for you," declares the LORD, "plans to prosper you and not to harm you, plans to give you hope and a future."

JEREMIAH 29:11 NIV

Trust God's Road Map

Sometimes I feel lost, Lord. I don't know which way to turn. Should I take this class or that class? Should I join this sport or that sport? Should I listen to this friend or that friend? It's all so confusing. There are times I wish I had a map to follow. That would sure make things easier. Then I remember that Your Word is a map! It gives me everything I need to make good decisions. So today I choose to open my Bible and lean on Your understanding, not my own. Be my guide, Lord. I'll gladly follow as long as You take the lead. You're the most trustworthy leader I could ever find, and I'm so happy to be tagging along behind You. Amen.

Trust in the LORD with all your heart and lean not on your own understanding; in all your ways submit to him, and he will make your paths straight.

PROVERBS 3:5–6 NIV

Talents, Gifts, Abilities

I'm having so much fun discovering my talents and abilities, Lord. I'm not always the most talented girl in the group, but I try! I pull out my dancing shoes in ballet class, stretch my fingers on the piano, swing a bat at softball practice, or swim laps on the swim team. I try lots of things and hope to discover what I'm really good at. I know You will help me find just the right talents to develop, Lord. And I know You're the One who gave me those talents in the first place. What will I be when I grow up? . . . A writer? A teacher? A missionary? A doctor? A singer? I'm not sure yet, but one day it will all be crystal clear. Until then, help me "grow my gifts" as I practice, practice, practice! Thanks for helping me dream, Lord. Amen.

As each has received a gift, use it to serve one another, as good stewards of God's varied grace.

1 PETER 4:10 ESV

Dreams

Lord, I have so many hopes and dreams! Sometimes I feel like a character in a fairy tale wondering if any of my wishes will come true. I know You're not a genie in a bottle, Lord, but I also know that You care a lot about my dreams. Which ones will come to pass? Only You know, Lord, but I know I can trust You. So as I think about things like what I want to be when I grow up or which part I want to get in the school play, I'll trust that You will bring the right things to pass. And I won't fret when things don't seem to be going my way, because I know that You will fulfill all the dreams that matter most. I trust You, Lord. Amen.

Commit your work to the LORD,
and your plans will be established.

PROVERBS 16:3 ESV

When I Can't See the Road

Sometimes it's hard not to get scared, Lord. Frightening things happen and my knees knock together, my hands shake, and my voice quivers. Oh boy, do I get the shivers! I'm so glad You tell me in Your Word that I don't have to be afraid even when the storm is blowing around me. I can trust in You even when I'm going through something super scary. Next time I'm tempted to curl up in a ball and hide from the world, give me courage. Take my hand and walk me through the crisis. Strengthen me from the inside out. I know I can get through anything as long as we are together, Lord. Thanks for helping me get rid of fear. Amen.

So do not fear, for I am with you; do not be dismayed, for I am your God. I will strengthen you and help you; I will uphold you with my righteous right hand.

ISAIAH 41:10 NIV

Making a Difference

I'm just one person. One girl. Sometimes I wonder if I can make a difference in this world. I overhear my parents talking about bad things happening—stuff they see on the news—and I see how many people are angry and upset. Some of it is really, really bad. But how can I fix things? I can't go anywhere or do anything. So maybe the only thing I can do is pray, Lord. I know You have the answers. So if I stop worrying—worry never helps anyway—then You can be in charge. Please help my parents to stop worrying too, Lord. They get so worked up when the bad stuff happens. Bring peace to our home and peace to our country, I pray. Amen.

Never stop praying, especially for others. Always pray by the power of the Spirit. Stay alert and keep praying for God's people.

EPHESIANS 6:18 CEV

Travel

Sometimes I wonder where I'll travel when I grow up. Will I go to the Amazon rain forest and see the monkeys and iguanas? Will I travel to Africa to see giraffes, elephants, and zebras? Will I go to the South Pole to visit penguins? Will I end up in Australia hanging out with koalas? All over this great big globe, there are places worth visiting. There are mountains and canyons, deserts and rivers, oceans and beaches galore. And I want to see them all. Thanks for creating this big, amazing planet, filled with wondrous places to explore, Lord. I can hardly wait to visit them! Amen.

The LORD will keep your going out and your coming in from this time forth and forevermore.

PSALM 121:8 ESV

The Future

Sometimes I wish I could see into the future, Lord. I'd like to know what I'm going to be when I grow up, and what I will look like. Will I get married? Have kids? If so, how many? What sort of job will I have? Will I still love the same things I love now, or will my tastes change? Who will my friends be? What will my house look like? Only You can see into the future, Lord. You know it all. I trust You to take care of me every step of the way. I won't be anxious about the future. I'll just look forward to it with great joy. Amen.

However, as it is written: "What no eye has seen, what no ear has heard, and what no human mind has conceived" —the things God has prepared for those who love him— these are the things God has revealed to us by his Spirit.

1 CORINTHIANS 2:9–10 NIV

You Go Ahead of Me

I have the best guide ever, Lord! You lead the way. I can almost picture it now: We're walking down a narrow road, and You're always one step ahead of me so I don't lose my way. We come to a fork in the road. For a minute, I'm confused about which way to go. Then You step to the right. . .and I follow behind You! You're a great leader, by the way! Though I can't see You with my eyes, I do sense Your presence when I pray, Lord, and I'm guided by Your Word. What an amazing Father You are, always taking me in just the right direction. I feel so safe with You. Amen.

Then the angel of the LORD went ahead and stood in a narrow place, where there was no way to turn either to the right or to the left.

NUMBERS 22:26 ESV

THE WORLD AROUND ME

There's a big, wide, wonderful world out there, and it's filled with people of every shape, size, and color. It's also teeming with nature's beauty—mountains, rivers, streams, and wildlife galore. Isn't it amazing to realize that the same God who created you also thought of all that?

Compassion

Sometimes I walk right by people and don't even realize they're hurting, Lord. I'm so focused on myself that I don't see. They are brokenhearted, and I don't even notice or care. Today when I see people in need, give me Your heart for them. I want to love them the way You do. I want to serve them the way You would serve them. I want to have a heart that truly cares for people in need. Give me Your compassion, Lord, so that I can stop focusing on me and truly love the very people who need me most. Point me in the right direction, I pray. Amen.

Be kind and compassionate to one another, forgiving each other, just as in Christ God forgave you.

EPHESIANS 4:32 NIV

Neighbors

I love living in a neighborhood, Lord. You placed people all around me. No matter where I live as I grow up—in a house, an apartment, or a townhouse—You surround me with people who can help. I want to be a good neighbor to those who live nearby. And I want to be a good neighbor and friend to those at church, at school, and at the playground. All of those people are like neighbors to me. Show me how to be kind and courteous to all of them and to love them as You love me. I know You love everyone the same, no matter what they look like or what kinds of jobs they have. Help me to love like You do, Lord. Amen.

Jesus replied: " 'Love the Lord your God with all your heart and with all your soul and with all your mind.' This is the first and greatest commandment. And the second is like it: 'Love your neighbor as yourself.' "

MATTHEW 22:37–39 NIV

The Ones I Never Meet

They're everywhere, Lord. I see them every day but never really get to know them. The mail carrier. The UPS guy. The lady who works the supermarket checkout. The man who hauls our trash away. They work so hard on my behalf, and I never say thanks. That doesn't seem fair. The next time I'm able, I want to thank some of those people for their hard work. I think it would brighten their day to hear a cheerful "Thanks!" every now and again. And while I'm at it, I think I'll pray for those people too! Everyone needs prayer. Thanks for the reminder that these people matter, Lord. They're awesome, and so are You. Amen!

Those who have served well gain an excellent standing and great assurance in their faith in Christ Jesus.

1 TIMOTHY 3:13 NIV

Admiration

There are so many people I admire, Lord. Some amazing women have poured themselves into my life—my grandmothers, my mom, ladies at church and in the neighborhood. Awesome men too. Thank You for these great people. I admire them so much. I want to be the kind of girl whom others admire—not because I wear pretty clothes or live in a great house, but because I actually care about others. When I live an others-focused life, that will happen, I know. I don't love people because I want to draw attention to myself, but because You love them. Above all, I admire You, Lord. You're the greatest example ever! Amen.

If I alone bear witness about myself, my testimony is not true. There is another who bears witness about me, and I know that the testimony that he bears about me is true.

JOHN 5:31–32 ESV

Red and Yellow, Black and White

Lord, You have the best imagination ever! I don't know how You came up with the idea of making people in all different colors, but I love it! No one is exactly like anyone else. We're all unique. It's so cool to think about, because Your Word says we're all created in Your image. Does that mean You're lots of different colors? I'm just curious. Best of all, we're all equal in Your sight. No matter what, You love me as much as every other kid on the planet. Thanks for making us all so different, Lord. What a great idea! Amen.

And they sang a new song, saying: "You are worthy to take the scroll and to open its seals, because you were slain, and with your blood you purchased for God persons from every tribe and language and people and nation."

REVELATION 5:9 NIV

Pets

I'm such an animal lover, Lord! Puppies, kittens, gerbils, hamsters, fish. . . I love them all. They make me smile. I love watching animal videos online and can't wait to grow up so I can fill my house with all the pets I want! What pet will I get first? I want to be the kind of girl who takes care of animals, who loves them and treats them well. Whatever pets You send my way—Chihuahuas, dachshunds, Persian kittens, goldfish, rabbits, or turtles—I promise to do my best to offer the food, affection, and tender loving care they need. That's what You do for me after all. I want to learn from the best, Father. Amen.

Your righteousness is like the mountains of God; your judgments are like the great deep; man and beast you save, O LORD.

PSALM 36:6 ESV

In the News

I see them in the news, Lord. They live on the other side of the world from me, but they need my prayers. They have no food. Their country is at war. They are hurting. It breaks my heart to see them hurting, Lord! I want to curl up in a ball and cry, but that won't do anything to help. I need to do something. I can't travel across the world right now, but I can pray. And maybe—just maybe—I can send money to help. Maybe I can support a missionary or help feed a child. Show me creative ways to raise money for this cause. I want to do something, not just watch on TV. Will You show me how I can be a blessing to those who are hurting? Amen.

"I led them with cords of human kindness, with ties of love. To them I was like one who lifts a little child to the cheek, and I bent down to feed them."

HOSEA 11:4 NIV

Community

I love living in a community, Lord. My neighborhood is really cool. There are kids my age and older people too. We're one big happy family! Sometimes we throw parties on holidays and special days. People cook hot dogs, and we drink lemonade. Sometimes we even have parades! That's a blast. Other times, we all hang out at the pool together. Living in a community is a lot of fun. It also makes me feel safe. I know that people all around me are there for me if I have a need. It's great to hang out with others, Lord. Thank You for my community! Amen.

They devoted themselves to the apostles' teaching and to fellowship, to the breaking of bread and to prayer. Everyone was filled with awe at the many wonders and signs performed by the apostles. All the believers were together and had everything in common.

ACTS 2:42–44 NIV

The Animal Kingdom

Lions and tigers and bears, oh my! This world is filled with animals, and I love all of them. I enjoy watching monkeys at the zoo, puppies playing in the backyard, kittens wrestling with a ball of yarn. I love movies about animals across this planet—zebras on the African plain and koalas in Australia. I know that human beings need to take care of all of Your creation, so show me what I can do to help, Lord. Will I one day be a vet, caring for sick pets? Or will I work in a zoo, caring for animals with TLC? Maybe I'll be a pet owner, taking care of a sweet dachshund puppy. Who knows! Oh wait. . .You know! You've got it all planned out. And one day I'll know too! Thanks, God, for giving me a love for the animal kingdom. Amen.

Whoever is righteous has regard for the life of his beast, but the mercy of the wicked is cruel.

PROVERBS 12:10 ESV

Nature Sings Your Praise

Is it true, Lord? Are the heavens singing right now? The Bible says they are! Your Word also says that if I don't praise You, the rocks and hills will cry out. Wow. I have to confess, I would really love to hear that. All of nature sings Your praise—from the lamb's "baa" to a puppy's bark. Every sound, every image, every motion, is all in praise to You. The next time I see a rushing river or pebbles rolling along in a stream, I'll remember that every teensy-tiny sound is an echo of praise. You thought of everything, Lord, and I'm so glad! Amen.

The heavens declare the glory of God; the skies proclaim the work of his hands. Day after day they pour forth speech; night after night they reveal knowledge.

PSALM 19:1–2 NIV

Trust

Have you ever wondered what it means to have faith? It means you place your trust in God, even when it doesn't seem to make sense. It's hard, sure. . .but definitely worth it. God won't ever let you down. He's completely trustworthy. And He wants to grow your faith so that you can believe that for the rest of your life.

In God I Trust

God, I know I can trust You with anything. When I'm uncertain, I trust in You. When I'm nervous about something at school or home, I trust You. When I'm afraid and my emotions begin to spiral out of control, I trust You. When I need to be rescued, I trust You will show up. God, You've always been my safe place. You have never let me down, and I know that You never will. You are with me today and always! Amen.

Trust in the LORD with all your heart, and do not lean on your own understanding.

PROVERBS 3:5 ESV

Hope

Sometimes I get my hopes up, Lord. I get so excited thinking about a gift I hope to receive, or a trip I plan to take, that it's hard to think about the tasks right in front of me. It's fun to be hopeful, but I've got to be careful not to put my trust in the wrong things. Sometimes I hope for the wrong things—selfish hopes. Give me Your perspective, Lord. I want to hope for the best—for a good life, godly friends, a healthy family, and plenty of people to love. Hoping isn't about me, myself, and I. It's about growing stronger and stronger in You. I love You, Lord! Amen.

May the God of hope fill you with all joy and peace in believing, so that by the power of the Holy Spirit you may abound in hope.

ROMANS 15:13 ESV

Victory

I love to win, Lord! I think everyone does. It's great when my sports team wins, or when I come in first in a school competition. But I'm learning that the best victory of all—far better than getting an A+ on a paper—is trusting in You. When I place my trust in You, even in the hard times, You always lead me to victory. When I'm feeling sick, You make me whole. When my heart is hurting, You bring peace and comfort. When I'm scared, You make me bold. I could never achieve these things on my own, Lord. I need You so much. I'll stick close, I promise! With Your hand in mine, I'll always be victorious! Amen.

But thanks be to God! He gives us the victory through our Lord Jesus Christ.

1 CORINTHIANS 15:57 NIV

Provision

Life is so great, Lord! Food seems to magically appear on the table. I have clothes to wear, shoes on my feet, a roof over my head. I know, I know. . .my parents work hard so we can have all this stuff. But I also know that You are our Provider. You made sure my dad got a good job. You guided my parents to buy the perfect-for-us house. You make sure I have the food I need every day and the car that my mom drives. Your Word, the Bible, promises that You will take care of us. If I ever doubt that You will provide, don't let me forget: You will supply every single need. That means I'll never have to worry about anything. I'm so grateful, Lord. Amen.

And my God will supply every need of yours according to his riches in glory in Christ Jesus.

PHILIPPIANS 4:19 ESV

Confidence

Lord, You know I'm not always confident. Sometimes I'm scared. When I have to stand up in front of the class and give a presentation. When it's my turn at bat. When I'm at the dentist's office. It's hard not to be afraid. But Your Word says I can be strong and confident when I place my trust in You, and not in myself. I really need that, Lord, because life isn't always easy. I have hard days—at school, at home, and even when I'm hanging out with my friends. Thank You for the reminder that I can be confident as long as I'm trusting You. Whew! That's a relief, Father! Amen.

Be on your guard; stand firm in the faith; be courageous; be strong. Do everything in love.

1 CORINTHIANS 16:13–14 NIV

Trusting God's Will

I don't always understand Your will, Father. Sometimes awful things happen, and I don't get it at all. I'm confused. When bad things happen to good people—when a person gets sick and has to go in the hospital, or when a friend's father dies—I'm confused. I want to ask, "Aren't You supposed to be good all the time, Lord? If You are, then why are bad things happening?" Still, I choose to trust You, because I know You'll never let me down. I don't have to understand everything, Lord. When I get to heaven, You'll show me all I need to know. For now, when things don't go the way I think they should, I won't get upset. I'll continue to live the way You want me to. I won't lose faith. I'll keep going. Amen.

"Your kingdom come, your will be done, on earth as it is in heaven."

MATTHEW 6:10 ESV

Miracles

I love reading stories in the Bible, Lord. I especially love the ones about Jesus healing sick people. I wish I could have been there to watch a blind man's eyes be opened or a lame man walk again. I wish I could've seen Lazarus be raised to life again or a deaf child hear for the first time. How cool would that be? I've read in Your Bible that You still perform miracles today. It would be amazing to see one firsthand. Maybe one day I'll watch You heal someone who's sick—a grandparent, a friend, or a teacher, perhaps. Until then, I look forward to that day. I thank You for still healing people in modern times. You think of everything, God! That's how much You care about Your kids. Wow, You're amazing! Amen.

"Behold, I will bring to it health and healing,
and I will heal them and reveal to them
abundance of prosperity and security."

JEREMIAH 33:6 ESV

Boldness

Lord, sometimes I feel a little shy. I see someone being hurt by others, and I don't say anything. I'm scared of what people will think. I want to speak up, but I don't have the courage. I want to hide in my room and keep to myself. It's easier than sharing what's on my mind. Help me become bolder, Father! Seriously! Give me the kind of power that only comes from You—superhero stuff! I don't want to be a fraidy cat anymore. I want to stick up for what's right and help those who need a friend. That can only happen if I'm bold. I need Your help, Lord, so I can help others. Amen.

"But you will receive power when the Holy Spirit comes on you; and you will be my witnesses in Jerusalem, and in all Judea and Samaria, and to the ends of the earth."

ACTS 1:8 NIV

Mustard Seed

My faith in You doesn't have to be huge, Lord. Your Word says all I need is faith the size of a teensy-tiny mustard seed. Wow! A mustard seed is like a little dot on a piece of paper. So even when I'm not feeling completely confident, all I need is a little bit of faith and You will move on my behalf. You'll move mountains if I speak to them. You'll perform miracles! Today I'm using my mustard seed faith. I'm speaking to the mountains in my life—the problems at school, friendship troubles, struggles with my emotions. . .all of it! I speak life and joy into those problems and can't wait to see You turn them around. Thank You in advance, Lord. Amen!

He replied, "If you have faith as small as a mustard seed, you can say to this mulberry tree, 'Be uprooted and planted in the sea,' and it will obey you."

LUKE 17:6 NIV

Trustworthiness

I don't like it when people let me down, Lord. They say we're going to do something together, then they back out at the last minute. Or they pretend to be my friend, only to turn their back on me later on. No matter how trustworthy or untrustworthy my friends are, there's one Friend who will never let me down. . .and that's You, Lord! If You say it, You'll do it. I won't ever have to wonder if You're going to back out on me. You'll be there, waiting. Teach me how to be trustworthy like You, Father. I want to be a girl who follows through and does what she says. Amen.

Moreover, it is required of stewards that they be found faithful.

1 CORINTHIANS 4:2 ESV

Blindfolded

Sometimes I feel like I've been blindfolded, Lord, like I don't know where to go or what to do. I can't see the signs because my eyes are covered. Then I remember that I can put my trust in You. With Your still, small voice, You will lead me. You know exactly which way to guide me. I can trust in You even when all else fails. When I'm in school and I'm confused about a test I'm taking, I'll listen to Your voice and trust You. When I'm hanging out with friends and one of them wants me to do something I shouldn't, I'll follow Your lead. I'm never really blind as long as You're with me, Lord. Thank You for being such a trustworthy leader! Amen.

Lead me in your truth and teach me, for you are the God of my salvation; for you I wait all the day long.

PSALM 25:5 ESV

Have you ever had a day when fantastic things happened right alongside horrible things? How is it possible to have both good and bad happen together? Some days are just like that. But here's the good news: God never changes. Whether you're up or down, God remains steady. You can hang on to Him.

The Roller Coaster

Lord, I don't get it. I thought today was going great. Things were really working out. Then all of a sudden—*bam!*—something terrible happened, something that shook me like an earthquake and upset everything, even the way I feel. I don't get it, Father. It's almost like I'm on a roller coaster, going up and down and all around. I need to feel settled. I don't want to feel like things are spinning out of control. So I'll hold on to You. I know You're my rock. You'll hold steady even when things around me are going crazy. I need You today, Lord. I'm holding tight to You! Amen.

He only is my rock and my salvation,
my fortress; I shall not be shaken.

PSALM 62:6 ESV

Real or Fake?

It's hard to tell if people are the real deal sometimes. I know You can see into their hearts, Lord. You know when they're faking it. But I only see the outside, and sometimes I fall for their tricks. I get drawn into situations, only to be hurt by the tricksters. Today, give me supernatural vision to see when people are up to no good so that I can avoid them. I want to be friendly to others, but I don't want to be hurt. So help me avoid the hurters. Give me wisdom to know how to respond when I see people faking it. Most of all, make me the real deal—a girl who truly loves You and loves people. I don't ever want to be a fake, Lord. Amen.

If anyone says, "I love God," and hates his brother, he is a liar; for he who does not love his brother whom he has seen cannot love God whom he has not seen.

1 JOHN 4:20 ESV

Worry

I'm still very young, Lord, but sometimes I feel like I have worry lines on my forehead. If I'm not careful, I'll be completely wrinkled before long! I worry and fuss a lot, especially over things I can't control. I don't know why I struggle with this so much. I know I should trust You in all things. Today, would You please help me lay down my worries? Show me how to let go so that You can take hold of my problems and handle them without me. Nothing is too big for You, Lord. You're an amazing Father who cares about my every need. Amen.

"Can any one of you by worrying add a single hour to your life?"

MATTHEW 6:27 NIV

Sadness

Lord, sometimes I go through hard times. My heart feels broken in two. I curl up in my bed and cry so hard I can barely breathe. I want to pull the covers over my head and hide away from the rest of the world until the pain is over. Father, during those hard times, thank You for wrapping Your arms around me. Thank You for brushing away my tears and telling me that everything is going to be okay. I don't know what I'd do if You didn't love me and care so much about what I'm going through. I'm so grateful for Your tender loving care, especially when I'm sad. Thank You, Lord. Amen.

"He will wipe away every tear from their eyes,
and there will be no more death, sadness, crying,
or pain, because all the old ways are gone."

REVELATION 21:4 NCV

Problem-Solving

I'm not great at fixing stuff, Lord—broken things or broken relationships. Problem-solving isn't my thing. Let's face it, sometimes I'm better at getting into trouble than getting out of it. But with Your help, I can become a great problem-solver. You're the best at fixing things, even things that don't look fixable. Today I ask You to give me supernatural problem-solving skills. When I feel stuck, whisper in my ear, *"Try this!"* or *"Try that!"* I know with Your help, I can get better at getting *out* of sticky situations rather than into them. Amen.

I pray that your love will keep on growing and that you will fully know and understand how to make the right choices. Then you will still be pure and innocent when Christ returns. And until that day, Jesus Christ will keep you busy doing good deeds that bring glory and praise to God.

PHILIPPIANS 1:9–11 CEV

The Report Card

I don't understand, Lord. I worked really hard this semester. Why do my grades keep going up and down? Some days, I feel like a good student. Other days, I feel like a loser. It makes no sense at all, but I'll keep doing the best I can. Please help me give it my all. I don't want to get discouraged or give up. If this is a test, I want to pass it! That can only happen if You keep me focused. Maybe one day this will all make sense, but for now I'll just trust You. Amen.

Whatever you do, work heartily, as for the Lord and not for men, knowing that from the Lord you will receive the inheritance as your reward. You are serving the Lord Christ.

COLOSSIANS 3:23–24 ESV

The Big Breakup

She was my best friend, Lord. My *very* best. I told her everything—my hopes, my dreams, my fears, my wishes. She knows me better than anyone, and I really thought I could trust her. Then she went behind my back and said something terrible about me. I found out about it by accident, and now I don't know what to do. Do I tell her that I know? Do I act like everything's cool when I know it's not? It feels horrible to have my bestie do this to me, but I do promise to forgive her. It's just going to take time. Will You help me through this, Lord? I'm totally confused and don't know what to do without Your help. Thanks, Lord. Amen.

Bearing with one another and, if one has a complaint against another, forgiving each other; as the Lord has forgiven you, so you also must forgive.

COLOSSIANS 3:13 ESV

Healing

I believe what the Bible says, Lord! You are a healer. You didn't just miraculously heal people back in Bible times; You're still healing people now. I can pray and believe! When someone I know is ill, I can trust their care to You. You're also a great heart-healer. When I'm brokenhearted or someone has hurt my feelings, You can wash away the pain. What an amazing God You are! Even when things don't go the way I hope—when someone I love passes away or when people make bad choices—I won't lose my faith, Lord. I still believe You want to see hearts and lives healed. Thank You for healing people today, Father. Amen.

So they set out and went from village to village, proclaiming the good news and healing people everywhere.

LUKE 9:6 NIV

The Big Move

This can't be happening, Lord. I thought we would live in this house. . .forever. My friends are here. My school is here. My life is here. Can it be possible that we have to move away? Will I really have to start again and make new friends in a brand-new part of the country? Mom finally got that new dishwasher she wanted, and I've got my room decorated perfectly. My brother is on a T-ball team and won't know what to do when we move away. Okay, deep breath. I'm going to trust You, Lord, even though none of this makes sense to me. I don't know where we're headed, but if You'll go with me, I know we'll be just fine. I'm holding tight to You, Lord! Amen.

For every house is built by someone,
but the builder of all things is God.

HEBREWS 3:4 ESV

Moving to a New School

Lord, it's so hard to be the new kid. I know You've experienced this too. When Jesus came as a babe in a manger, He was the new kid in town. And He wasn't always accepted or appreciated. That's kind of how I feel when I go to a new school or church. No one really knows me. And sometimes it feels like they don't want to take the time to get to know me. They already have their own groups, and I'm not a member of the club. Help me find my perfect fit, Lord! Show me the girls You want me to be friends with. Help me to get settled in, no matter how hard it is. I might be a little nervous, but I'm so excited about what the future holds! Amen.

Fear not, for I am with you; be not dismayed, for I am your God; I will strengthen you, I will help you, I will uphold you with my righteous right hand.

ISAIAH 41:10 ESV

DISCOVERIES

There are so many exciting discoveries yet to be made in your life. So many adventures to go on. Already you're learning life lessons at every turn. (You're an amazing student, by the way.) Before this journey is over, you'll be a regular whiz kid, filled with knowledge!

Boundaries

I didn't really understand the word *boundaries* when I was little, Lord. Now I get it! There are boundaries—rules and limits—to keep me safe. When I cross those boundaries, dangerous things can happen. So I choose to live within the boundaries You've given me in Your Word. I'll obey my parents, love others, and respect the people You've placed in authority in my life—my grandparents, teachers, police officers, church leaders, and so on. I'll obey the law and follow the rules, because I know my life will be blessed when I do. Thanks for boundaries, Lord. I'm so glad You keep me safe and sound. Amen.

Let your foot be seldom in your neighbor's house,
lest he have his fill of you and hate you.

PROVERBS 25:17 ESV

It's Just Stuff

I have so much stuff, Lord. It fills my room. Electronics, toys, games, stuffed animals, clothes, shoes. . .*whew!* Sometimes I have *so* much stuff that it fills up the room and I can barely step over it. That's when I know it's time to cut back. Show me which things I can get rid of—give to children in need or toss in the trash—so I only have what I truly need. I don't want to be a collector of stuff. I want to have room in my life for the things that truly matter. Time to clean things up, Lord! Amen.

"Do not lay up for yourselves treasures on earth, where moth and rust destroy and where thieves break in and steal, but lay up for yourselves treasures in heaven, where neither moth nor rust destroys and where thieves do not break in and steal. For where your treasure is, there your heart will be also."

MATTHEW 6:19–21 ESV

The Holy Spirit's Voice

I can hear Your voice, Lord! Through Your Spirit, You speak to my heart. You whisper words of comfort when I'm hurting. You say things like, *"Peace, be still!"* And when I'm angry, You calm me with words like, *"Calm down."* I don't know if I'll ever hear Your voice with my ears, but for now, go on speaking to my heart. I need Your wisdom and Your guidance, especially when I'm at school or hanging out with my friends. I want to be a girl who knows Your voice, one who listens and then obeys. Thanks for speaking to me, Lord. Amen.

As He spoke to me the Spirit entered me and set me on my feet; and I heard Him speaking to me.

EZEKIEL 2:2 NASB

Accepting Yourself

It's a lot of fun to open a present, Lord. . .to peek inside and see a beautiful gift. Sometimes I forget that I am a present to those around me. I am beautiful in their sight and in Yours. I don't feel beautiful sometimes, Father. When I look in the mirror, I see all the things I wish I could change—my chubby cheeks, my freckles, my hair, even my height. Today, please help me to accept myself. I want to remember that I'm a gift, and I was created in Your image. Thank You for wrapping me up with ribbons and bows and placing me in my family. I don't ever want to forget that! May I learn to love and accept myself as You do. Amen.

I praise you, for I am fearfully and wonderfully made. Wonderful are your works; my soul knows it very well.

PSALM 139:14 ESV

Emotions

Lord, I'm so glad You created emotions. Whether I'm happy (Yay!) or sad (Boo!), I know I can count on You to see me through what I'm feeling. Sometimes I cry when my heart is heavy (Ugh!), but other times I want to dance for joy (Yippee!). Sometimes I laugh until I can't see straight; other times I feel so happy I can barely hold it in! I'm so glad You knew in advance that I would need these emotions, Father. And how great to know that You have feelings too. The Bible says there's a time for every emotion—crying, laughing, mourning, and dancing. You get it, Lord. I'm an emotional girl. . .and that's okay. Amen.

A time to weep, and a time to laugh;
a time to mourn, and a time to dance.

ECCLESIASTES 3:4 ESV

Pride

It's one thing to be proud of a football team, Lord. It's another thing to be so proud of yourself that you think you're better than everyone else. I see people do this all the time. They think they're better at sports or better at singing—stuff like that. Or maybe they think they're better because of the color of their skin or where they go to school. People get prideful about a lot of things. Only You can erase pride, Lord. Only You can tell people that they need to treat others the way they want to be treated. Start right here, right now, I pray. If there's any pride inside of me, I ask You to wipe it away, Lord. I want to care more about others than myself. Amen.

Don't be jealous or proud, but be humble and consider others more important than yourselves. Care about them as much as you care about yourselves and think the same way that Christ Jesus thought.

PHILIPPIANS 2:3–5 CEV

Promises

I know You never break Your promises, Lord. If You said it, You will do it. Me? I break promises all the time. Oh, I don't mean to, but I do. I tell Mom I'm going to clean my room, then I don't follow through. I tell my kid sister I'll hang out with her but end up spending time with my friends instead. I promise my dad that I'll do better at guarding my temper, then I slip up and yell at my brother again. Yep, I'm ashamed to admit it, but sometimes I'm a promise-breaker, not a promise-keeper. But with Your help, I can get better. I can be a girl who follows through, who does what she says. Thanks for helping me with this, Lord! Amen.

In view of all this, make every effort to respond to God's promises. Supplement your faith with a generous provision of moral excellence, and moral excellence with knowledge.

2 PETER 1:5 NLT

Listening

I know, I know! I should talk less and listen more. I've been told many times, Lord. I've even been called a chatterbox. I try to hold my tongue, but it's so hard! There's just so much I want to say, and I get super excited to get my words out. From now on, I'm going to try to be a better listener. I know there are other people out there who want to get their words out too. So I'll zip my lips and open my ears. I'll pay close attention and not interrupt. I just might learn something amazing if I listen instead of talk. Will You help me with this, Lord? It's not going to be easy. Boy, do I ever need Your help with this one! Amen.

Know this, my beloved brothers: let every person be quick to hear, slow to speak, slow to anger.

JAMES 1:19 ESV

As You Love Yourself

Lord, I've read in the Bible that You want me to love other people the way I love myself. I'll be honest—I mostly put myself first. I eat what I like, dress in clothes I like, and do the things I love to do—like play with my friends. I think what You're trying to tell me is that I should love other people like that—to make sure they are happy and have what they need. I should stop focusing on me and spend more time focusing on others. But it's also kind of cool to know that it's okay to love myself. I guess it makes sense. If I didn't love myself, I probably wouldn't take care of myself—eat good foods, get good sleep, brush my teeth, that sort of stuff. So I'll do my best to take care of me. . .*and* others. Amen.

" 'Love the Lord your God with all your heart and with all your soul and with all your mind.' This is the first and greatest commandment. And the second is like it: 'Love your neighbor as yourself.' "

MATTHEW 22:37–39 NIV

Love Is the Greatest

I sometimes wonder if I can stick to the rules, Lord. I mess up a lot. That's why I'm glad that the greatest commandment, or rule, is to love You and love people. Even when I mess up, which is a lot, my love for You never changes. And I know Your love for me never goes away either. And You know I'll always love the people in my life—my parents, siblings, and friends. It's amazing to think about how powerful Your love is. It erases sins, makes friends out of enemies, and even causes wars to come to an end. If I haven't told You in a while, I really, truly love You, Lord. You've made my life so awesome. I'm going to spend the rest of my life letting others know about Your amazing, powerful love. Amen.

And now these three remain: faith, hope and love. But the greatest of these is love.

1 CORINTHIANS 13:13 NIV

Old Testament

New Testament

1 CORINTHIANS

2 CORINTHIANS

GALATIANS

EPHESIANS

PHILIPPIANS